THE SPIRIT OF SILENCE

Reviews of other books by John Lane:

Timeless Simplicity: Creative Living in a Consumer Society
"In keeping with its title, this is a straightforward book, beautifully illustrated, well ordered, with clear directions and useful references. What is more, it is written without cant, and, most importantly, not by a zealot but by a practitioner. Only someone who has sought to practise the simple life would know its detail, the small matters that make it so."—David Cadman, *Resurgence*

Timeless Beauty: In the Arts and Everyday Life
"This is a vital book for the renewal of Western civilisation"—*Scientific & Medical Network*

"John Lane challenges us to stop and consider just how important and vital to our health and happiness beauty actually is. . . . This beautifully written and researched book provides an important missing piece in understanding the cultural and environmental crises facing the world today"—Terry Irwin, *Resurgence*

The Living Tree: Art and the Sacred
"It is heartening that a working painter has spoken out against the stupidity and obscurantism that has disfigured much modernism in art . . . Lane is telling us that art can still regenerate, can still lead us towards the sacred and the ineffable. The basis of his work is to 'give praise'. *The Living Tree* marks an important point in the history of art criticism which has lain dormant since Ruskin. It builds upon the pioneer work done by Titus Burckhardt in *Sacred Art East and West*, and Coomaraswamy's studies on the traditional artist. It is a courageous attempt to reaffirm the transcendental as the true repository of artistic expression."—James Cowan, author of *Mysteries of the Dreamtime*

"John Lane summons our culture back to abiding values."—Kathleen Raine, *Temenos*

"This book gives us an almost total picture of the power and magnificence of art in all its facets. From the title one may have thought that it was an ecological book urging us to preserve the tropical rainforest, but from the sub-title one will realise that it is the living tree of being and becoming."—Stefan Valouski, *New Humanity*

"I found *The Living Tree* articulate, erudite and inspiring."—Gay Smith, *One Earth*

A Snake's Tail Full of Ants: Art, Ecology and Consciousness

"I loved *The Living Tree*, but the new one is even better. It is the best book I have ever read on what we might refer to as the philosophy of art."—Edward Goldsmith, author of *The Way: An Ecological Worldview* and co-author of *The Case Against the Global Economy*

"I began dipping into this ominously titled book and ended reading every word. I was riveted by the author's analysis, his uncompromising clarity and his shrewdness of exposition . . . It is impossible for anyone to read it without being enriched."—John Papworth, *Fourth World Review*

"I urge people to read *A Snake's Tail Full of Ants* and enjoy its rich territory."—Denys Trussell, *The Ecologist*

"Anyone concerned with the overt betrayal of art in our time, anyone concerned with the vital relationship between spirit, community, nature and art will find *A Snake's Tail Full of Ants* rewarding . . . It could be put with great advantage alongside Gombrich's *The Story of Art*. There can be little doubt that many young people . . . would find this book something of a revelation."—Peter Abbs, *Temenos Academy Review*

The

Spirit of Silence

Making space for creativity

John Lane

with illustrations by Clifford Harper

Chelsea Green Publishing Company
White River Junction, Vermont

First published in 2006
by Green Books Ltd
Foxhole, Dartington
Totnes, Devon TQ9 6EB
www.greenbooks.co.uk

Published in the United States by
Chelsea Green Publishing Company
PO Box 428
White River Junction, VT 05001
802-295-6300
www.chelseagreen.com

Design by Rick Lawrence
samskara@onetel.com

ISBN 1-903998-74-3

Also by John Lane:

New Directions: Ways of Advance for the Amateur Theatre
Arts Centres: Every Town should Have One
The Living Tree: Art and the Sacred
A Snake's Tail Full of Ants: Art, Ecology and Consciousness
In Praise of Devon: A Guide to its People, Places and Character
Timeless Simplicity: Creative Living in a Consumer Society
Timeless Beauty: In the Arts and Everyday Life

Contents

Acknowledgements

I want to thank those friends who read my manuscript and helped me to improve it. These include Satish Kumar for his inspiration, companionship and comments on an early draft and Harland Walshaw who edited the manuscript. His observations were insightful and especially invaluable. I am also grateful to Lorna Haworth, Philip Mann, Roger Hill, and the staff at Torrington Library, for further assistance. To David Cadman I also offer heartfelt thanks for his contribution to the theme of silence. Further thanks must go to my publisher, John Elford, for his personal and professional support. And finally, to my wife, Truda, to whom I owe everything. Without her unselfish and loving support I should not have been able to write the book.

For my children & grandchildren

The present state of the world and the whole of life is diseased.
If I were a doctor and were asked for my advice, I should reply:
Create silence! Bring men to silence!

SØREN KIERKEGAARD

Elected Silence, sing to me
And beat upon my whorlèd ear,
Pipe me to pastures still and be
The music that I care to hear.

GERARD MANLEY HOPKINS

Silence is nothing merely negative; it is not
the mere absence of speech. It is
a positive, a complete world in itself.

Silence has greatness simply because it is.
It is, and that is its greatness, its pure existence.

There is no beginning to silence and no end:
it seems to have its origins in the time when everything
was still pure Being. It is like uncreated, everlasting Being.

When silence is present, it is as though nothing but silence
had ever existed. . . . It is the only basic phenomenon
that is always at man's disposal. . . No other basic phenomenon
is so present in every moment as silence.

MAX PICARD

Introduction

Silence touches us in many different ways: as something which offers sanctuary and tranquillity, as something which brings us into touch with the inner depths which elude us in the hurly-burly of our everyday lives, as a source of joy, as as an inspiration for art, literature or music, and because it awakens us to the present moment which can only be fully experienced with a mind that is free of preconceptions. These encounters can be the source of a wonderful clarity.

"No man will ever unfold the capacities of his own intellect who does not at least chequer his life with solitude," wrote Thomas De Quincy; but solitude is more than intellect. It is a therapeutic support, an anchor to reality. It is the source of imagination, vision and philosophic insight. The many poets, artists, philosophers and inventors who spent the greater part of their lives alone and in silence are countless. There are Newton, Pascal and Wittgenstein. There are Monteverdi, Bach, and our contemporaries, Sofia Gubaidulina and Arvo Pärt—who is composing music, according to one commentator, which is "the most beautiful sound next to silence". It is also true of the Buddha meditating on the banks of the Nairanjana river, Jesus in the wilderness, the Prophet Mohammed in the cave of Mount Hera, Lao-Tse in the mountains of China, and all the European mystics—Julian of Norwich, St Bernard of Clairvaux, Meister Eckhart, St Francis of Assisi, amongst others. It is no less true of certain European painters—Piero della Francesca, Vermeer, Corot, Caspar David Friedrich and Morandi—whose work is imbued with the profoundest silence. No less is true of the creators of the interior spiritual beauty of the Orthodox icon which reflects the glory and beauty of God and His saints. The poet Coleridge said that deep feeling was only possible with deep thought, and I'd add: great silence.

But of course the value of solitude and silence is not limited to mystics, artists and philosophers; nor is the contemplative life limited to those searching for God. No, the search for solitude and interior freedom belongs to all those who seek their own truth. One such was Admiral Byrd who single-handedly manned an advanced weather base in the Antarctic during the winter of 1934. In his diary for 14 April he writes:

> Took my daily walk at 4 p.m. today in 89 degrees of frost . . . I paused to listen to the silence . . . The day was dying, the night being born—but with great peace. Here were imponderable processes and forces of the cosmos, harmonious and soundless. Harmony, that was it! That was what came out of the silence—a gentle rhythm, the strain of a perfect chord, the music of the spheres perhaps.
>
> It was enough to catch the rhythm, momentarily to be myself a part of it. In that instant I could feel no doubt of man's oneness with the universe.

Our early ancestors were almost certainly in close touch with that harmony of the cosmos which Admiral Byrd experienced in the Antarctic. Why is this so? Because, I believe, they were more familiar with the peace of solitude and the serenity of silence than we are today. Our noisy, energetic culture makes both of these difficult to attain. And the belief that success in intimate personal relationships is the key to happiness ignores the creative value of being alone.

This book is for those who, like myself, cherish solitude and value timelessness. It is for those who wish to deepen the stream of their lives; for those who seek to gain an entry into pure existence, and are prepared to jettison some of the conditioning and junk of modern life in order to find it.

The importance of emptying the mind has been recognised for millennia; in Buddhist societies, meditation is a way of life for millions. In the fourth and last stage of their life, the Hindu renounces all worldly attachments for a life of contemplation, asceticism and seclusion. In Japan, the tea ceremony provides an interlude of stillness in lives otherwise rooted in activity. But the quest for solitude, tranquillity and love of nature is not limited to the East. As we shall see, Europeans like Henry David Thoreau, the painter Paul Cézanne and the Catholic monk Thomas Merton were dramatic, if unusual, cases of the universal human exploration of new ways of being.

These were people of an exceptional kind, but most of us in a more private manner will also sometimes search for the succour of silence and stillness in our lives. It may be stroking the cat, pottering in the garden, praying, meditating, listening to music or simply gazing at the waves of an incoming sea, but we do these things because we find them replenishing; just as a field benefits from lying fallow so we can benefit from periods of uninterrupted rest. That part of ourselves which demands something more than vacuity and shallow sensationalism deserves our time and respect.

It is my hope that this book, a sequel to *Timeless Simplicity: creative living in a consumer society*, will encourage more of us to give solitude and stillness an honoured and essential place in their lives.

CHAPTER ONE

Spiritual Space

Fish live in shoals, bees fly in swarms, but some animals—domestic cats, for example—are solitary. Humans mix the two: we are both gregarious and solitary. We live in families, in tribes and in cities, yet at the same time we enjoy the comfort of sometimes being alone. We garden, we read or pray by ourselves. Even if we spend most of our time with others, there are periods when we enjoy our own company more. We choose to retreat from the bustle of the world to find our own 'space'. Here silence has a healing effect. Here solitude helps bring my fundamental sense of who I am into focus. In silence and solitude we find both the time and space to enjoy in tranquillity, the timeless wonder of consciousness: the miracle of, say, a bank of wild garlic or a greater spotted woodpecker in flight. As Ronald Blythe observes, noise causes us to hear very little; silence makes us hear wonderful sounds.

Silence was once valued. The quest for solitude dates back to ancient times, with roots in Chinese, Indian and Western philosophies. From Lao-Tse and Buddha, the Desert Fathers and the early Celtic hermits, through Rousseau, Henry David Thoreau and Thomas Merton to the present day, certain individuals have rejected the materialism of their societies in favour of simplicity and the quest for spiritual wisdom. They have travelled to find solitude. They have listened to silence and heard therein their own creative heartbeat. Exposed to stillness, they have learnt what lies deepest in themselves. Indeed, the person who dares to be alone can come to experience that which is unhindered by experience, craving or prejudice. The truth of this can only be found by the practice itself, and even then it cannot be expressed in words.

Silence comes from the unseen, the beyond, and to experience it is to come into contact with the beginnings of things, to be made new. As Thomas Merton says, "The solitary, far from enclosing himself in himself, becomes every man. He dwells in the solitude, the poverty, the indigence of every man."

In most of the pre-industrial past, silence was everywhere. Richard Rolle of Hampole (c.1300–1349), the father of English mysticism, wrote extolling its numerous virtues: "Great liking I had in wilderness to sit, that I far from noise sweetlier might sing, and with quickness of heart likingest praising I might feel; the which doubtless of his gift I have taken, Whom all things wonderfully I have loved."

No longer is silence to be found everywhere. Our age is hostile to silence, and with it, to reverence for nature. Even in the part of Britain where I live, designated one of the country's least noisy areas, the clatter of quickening stimuli now overlays the older world of peace. The countryside of north Devon is rarely silent, and less dark than it used to be. The hum of transport, particularly of aeroplanes, the sound of machinery, provides a constant drone; in Exeter, the county town, it is deafening. In the shops, the restaurants, the bars, the streets, even the vets and opticians, amplified 'music' runs as uninterruptedly as a washerless tap. There is no silence any longer.

People want noise and light; they abhor their absence. But that is not all; we also crave unceasing entertainment and stimulation. Alongside noise, moving pictures, news items, magazines, food, drink, clothing, drugs, anti-depressants, travel, sexual partners and, of course, money, are all consumed. To adapt some words of George Orwell: Ours is a restless, cultureless life, centring around convenience foods, the television set, the computer game and the mobile phone. It is a civilisation in which children grow up with an intimate knowledge of Star Wars and in complete ignorance of the Bible. To that civilisation belong the people who are most at home in, and most definitely of, the modern world: the technicians and the higher paid skilled workers, the experts in IT, rock stars, footballers, and compères of some of the most popular entertainment on television.[1]

Orwell was describing a society in which we have become cogs in an out-of-control economic wheel, a value system that does not see people as human beings but as consumers of *things*. Everything declares it: the commercials on television, the huge billboards advertising cars, the junk mail promoting foreign travel, the adverts on the World Wide Web—words, images, sounds, conduct, all telling the same story. Interestingly enough, the Buddha reviled the very characteristics—sensual desire, craving, restlessness, discontent, longing for gain—which these commercials either seek to satisfy or extol. The classical deadly sins—avarice, envy, lust, gluttony, pride and sloth—have long ceased to be condemned; with the exception of anger, their practice is supportive of the market economy.

Critics of capitalism are legion, but perhaps few have got closer to the truth than the eminent German-born social psychiatrist, Erich

Fromm (1900–80). The average person, he argues, is now a stranger in the universe; at the deepest level he senses his depression and boredom, the emptiness that pervades his soul. It is this emptiness and dissaffection which demand satisfaction and filling by noise, possessions and entertainment. Yet, as we all know, noise and entertainment make us still emptier and needier. They do not make us happier.

> All our amusements serve the purpose of making it easy for him to run away from himself and from the threatening boredom by taking refuge in the many ways of escape which our culture offers him; yet covering up a symptom does not do away with the conditions which produce it. Aside from the fear of physical illness, or of being humiliated by the loss of status and prestige, the fear of boredom plays a paramount role among the fears of modern man. In a world of fun and amusement, he is afraid of boredom and glad when another day has passed without mishap, another hour has been killed without his having become aware of the lurking boredom.

These words were written in the early sixties, at a time before the advent of global warming and the current vandalism of our earthly inheritance; before, that is, the despoliation of the planet of which we are becoming ever more conscious. So to Fromm's despair over the killing of the hours we can now add the killing of all life on Earth. Yet the extinction of the amphibians, mammals, birds and fish, our unfulfilled bid to abate our enormous hunger for stimulation and the enthusiasm for materialism are all related; they are a unity. As the Buddhist philosopher Dr Daisaku Ikeda has written: "A barren destructive mind produces a barren, devastated environment. The desertification of the planet is created by the desertification of the human spirit."

So silence and solitude have never been more important. They preserve us from exhaustion, from fanaticism, from restlessness—from excess. They remain the fertile ground of creation, the source of contemplation, the place of mindfulness and, between two lovers so at ease with one another that they don't need to fill the space around them with conversation, of intimate communion. It is only in solitude and silence that our life is really present, that we are truly responsive to the heartbeat of the universe and free to contemplate the miracle of existence. Not, perhaps, the world of the street but the world of the *now*.

So let us begin this journey by *looking at* the astonishing wonder of creation and by *listening to* the subtle polyphony of the sounds which surround us—the sight of the clouds above the rooftop, the rustle of leaves on the pavement, the scrape of a spoon on the surface of a china bowl, the footstep of the cat climbing the stairs.

Treading the path of solitude and silence can liberate us from a life of agitation and take us towards a serene awareness of the present moment. It can bring us from a life of indulgent consumerism and unreflective conformity to the springs of being: the naked realisation and acceptance of other people and things for what they are. "It is in solitude," writes Isabel Colgate, "that the self meets itself, or, if you like, its God, and from there that it goes out to join the communal dance. No amount of group therapy, study of interpersonal relationships, self-improvement exercises, personal training in the gym, can assuage the loneliness of those who cannot bear to be alone."

Is it surprising that silence lies at the heart of all the great religions and, no less, the creation of so much thought, prayer, art, music and literature?

CHRISTIAN SILENCE

That language should be so very important in houses of silence is a paradox of monasteries. They are houses of the soul, and their deepest language comes from the depth of silence.
Peter Levi

Vocation to Solitude—to deliver oneself up, to hand oneself over, entrust oneself completely to the silence of a wide landscape of woods and hills, or sea, or desert; to sit still while the sun comes up over that land and fills its silences with light. To pray and work in the morning and to labour and rest in the afternoon, and to sit still again in meditation in the evening when night falls upon that land and when the silence fills itself with darkness and with stars. This is a true and special vocation. There are few who are willing to belong completely to such silence, to let it soak into their bones, to breathe nothing but silence, to feed on silence, and to turn the very substance of their life into a living and vigilant silence.
Thomas Merton

The eremite is a person who lives in solitude, retreating from the bustle of the world and human company to concentrate on religious devotion. The word *hermit* is derived from the Greek word meaning 'desert'; the word *monk* comes from the Greek meaning 'alone'; both varieties have been known in different forms in every civilisation. Hinduism, Buddhism and Taoism have their holy men and women. Many Chinese landscape paintings show solitary hermits in reclusion from the world of humanity.

Christianity, too, has inspired people to leave the world for a life of prayer and self-imposed hardship. Very early in its history, certain individuals began to move away from what they regarded as the wickedness and luxury of the world to seek God in the solitary desert. The Judaic, Islamic and Christian faiths flowered from roots which had been struck in desert sand.

There were recluses from about 313 AD, the time that Constantine recognised the new Christian faith. The most famous of these was St Antony, generally regarded as the father of monasticism. Having given away his possessions, he found a hard life in a city still too distracting, and withdrew into the Egyptian desert in 285. Here he remained, battling demons for a further twenty years, living on bread, salt and water, fasting for three or four days at a time and going without sleep for longer periods. Such austerities appear to be characteristic of those seeking a genuine holiness. Solitude, poverty, obedience, silence and prayer dispose the soul for its mysterious destiny in God.

But Antony was not alone. In 394 a traveller reported that there were almost as many monks in the desert as there were citizens in the towns. There were said to be 5,000 monks at Mount Nitria, 10,000 at Arsinoe, and 7,000 men and women at Tabenna in the Nile Valley. However exaggerated these figures may be, and the stories of the asceticism of the Desert Fathers, we should not allow this to detract from the sincerity of their quest. The significance of their endeavours is not to be found in their penchant for sleeplessness and flagellation, but in their reaching for the infinite and their scorn for the mundane pursuits with which it is all too easy to dissipate the days.

In the 4th century the monastic movement began to spread into Western Europe. In 527 St Benedict formed his monastery at Monte Cassino in northern Italy and drew up the Rule of St Benedict, the pattern of Western monastic life ever since. In this, Benedict made the typical Roman contribution of order and discipline, adding to poverty and chastity the rule of obedience.

The life he regulated was well balanced. Prayer and praise were its basis: the periods of worship, the canonical hours, occupied a little over two hours. Four to six hours were given to manual work in field or kitchen. Three hours were fixed as a minimum for study: "A cloister without books," he wrote, "is a fort without armoury." In addition, the canonical hours were embellished by the long-breathed, majestic chanting of the psalms in which every monk, however 'unmusical', shared. Thus work and prayer, music and study, community and solitude were conceived as a harmonious whole. The communal and the personal were integrated; neither too much nor too little of either. Poverty and charity were also important, the monk possessing nothing as an individual but given what was needed in order to live. Buildings and lands were held as common property. Yet poverty was not simply a question of possessions but a state of mind. It meant a release from preoccupation with material things in order to be able to concentrate on the things not of this world.

I have chosen to dwell on the pattern of monastic life because it is so strikingly at variance with the hectic restlessness of the modern age, yet characteristic of the infinite, eternal, transcendent mystery of being, which is the Ground of all religion. For those not seeking to enter a monastery, for those not even wishing to subscribe to the Catholic religion or, for that matter, any other faith, silence provides an alternative; pure silence rising from the depths of being carries us closer not only to what the Christian calls God but to what the agnostic recognises as a different stage of holiness, the holiness of enlightenment.

My own experience of the monastic life has been necessarily superficial, but from once frequent visits to the Benedictine abbeys of Solesmes and Quarr on the Isle of Wight I have experienced something of that "healing and mysterious enchantment" of which Patrick Leigh Fermor wrote in his book on the monastic life, *A Time to Keep Silence*.

Quarr is not like the Trappist Order, a place of absolute silence, but nonetheless a kind of timelessness pervades its spirit and its walls. Behind the unhurried routine of each day—lunch in the refectory (eaten in silence); compline in the church or the *lectio divina* (sacred reading)—there is, like the ground bass in a suite by Bach, an undisturbed and fundamental human quietude. I say human because the natural world is rarely completely silent: the ice creaks, a waterfall roars, birds sing and the rain hisses, but we humans can, if we choose, be as peaceful as a plank of wood or a block of granite. "We must always remember that silence, solitude and prayer are the most important elements in the monastic life," writes Thomas Merton in his book on the subject, *The Silent Life*. In a monastery this silence, far from being a void, acts as a crucible for the manifold activities designed to transform the men and women who have chosen to make the inward journey within its walls. How different from the way we conduct our lives today!

The scale of the development of Christian monasticism in the European middle ages remains one of the miracles of Western civilisation; thousands of people were touched by its luminous spirit and influenced by the purity of its ideals. At the heart of many valleys and cities, a realm of silence prevailed. And by the end of the 13th century, at its peak, the Cistercian Order consisted of 700 abbeys, while the other major Orders—the Benedictine, Carthusian and Franciscan— were no less ubiquitous. In the 14th century there were 1,000 monastic houses in England. For a while the silent life, far from being rare, was the nourishing kernel of the life of the time. Silence, after all, was and is the great antidote; the great healer. It was the silence of the desert that 'saved' Western civilisation from the time of Constantine onwards; it was the silence of monasticism which forged a culture that, in another thousand years, gave birth to the modern West.

HINDU SILENCE

Find the eternal object of your quest
within your soul
Yaajur Veda

In contrast to the interior nature of the Christian monastery, the Hindu temple is a noisy place: it resounds with a pulsating vitality—colourful, sensuous and loud. On entering, the worshipper clangs the temple bell to alert the resident deity to his presence. Then the food offerings, the incense, the flowers, the lights, the chanting and hymnody all over-power and delight the senses. Yet even in this robust faith (not one cod-ified religion but a compilation of hundreds, perhaps thousands, of smaller belief systems) there is to be found the profoundest stillness. Hinduism encourages individuals who are so inclined to live as hermits and ascetics and spend their lives devoted to renunciation and contem-plation. They are called *sadhus* or *sannyasis*. It is estimated that there are more than 5 million sadhus and sannyasis in India. Ninety per cent of them are men.

According to Hindu doctrines, the ideal life consists of four stages: *brahmacarya*, the period of discipline and education, followed by *garhasthya*, the productive, procreative life of the householder fulfilling his duties to family and caste alike. In the the third stage, *vanaprasthya*, the 'twice-born' retires to the jungle to lead the life of a forest hermit, performing the fire-sacrifices and reciting the scriptures. In the final stage, the sadhu renounces all and becomes a wandering *sannyasa*, to seek union with the Divine, Brahman.

Sadhus and sannyasis vary greatly; there are those who live as her-mits in the mountains, entirely naked and covered in ashes, and those who live in relative comfort in large monasteries. Traditionally, their only possessions are a cotton loincloth, a begging bowl, a staff, some prayer beads, and the symbols of their deity—a trident for the Shaivas (disciples of the God, Shiva) or a conch for the Vaishnavas (disciples of the God Vishnu).

Ascetics come from every walk of life. It is not uncommon to encounter those who had been musicians, professors and even business-men in an earlier stage of their lives. Near Rishikesh, I met a delightful man who had lived in a cave, the cave of Nasist Gurfa, since 1934. He told me than in those days it had been surrounded by a forest inhabited by wild animals. As he sat in silent meditation, lions would visit him.

Meditation, puja, the practice of yoga, magico-religious rituals and the worship of a tutelary deity are the sadhu's commonest activities, each aimed at purification of the self. By practising such demanding vows of self-denial and even bodily torture, sadhus and sannyasis give proof of their dedication to the Divine. Yet whatever their choice of dedication, the primary aim of all Hindu ascetics is the honouring of the sacred. Sweeping the floor, taking a bath or cooking food are further evidence of their humility and deep dedication to the Divine.

But for the ordinary Hindu, the housewife and agricultural worker, the mother and street cleaner, the teacher and stall owner, dedication to the Divine may take the form of *Darsan*. Darsan means 'seeing'. In the Hindu ritual tradition it refers especially to religious seeing, or visual perception of the sacred. The central act of Hindu worship, from the point of view of the lay person, is to stand in the presence of the deity. The worshipper enters the temple, he or she beholds the image—be it Shiva or Parvati, Durga or Saraswati—and in that simple, contemplative act of seeing, is worshipping; through the eyes he or she gains the blessings of the divine. Surrounded by clamour, the ringing of bells, the offering of oil lamps, the eating of consecrated food, the pouring of milk and water, the comings and goings of other worshippers, our worshipper stands in a pool of silence. He is alone in a crowd; she is silent amongst noise. The incense, the flowers, the lights, the chanting and hymnody and food offerings are important, but the kernel of the religious experience in those moments is contained in the peace and blessings experienced by the devotee.

THE SILENCE OF ZEN

> Among the great things which are to be found among us, the Being of Nothingness is the greatest.
> *Leonardo da Vinci*

Whenever I remember India I am reminded of noise (and smells and colours), but when my mind turns to Japan, I think of silence. At one time (and that was before the influence of American culture), silence had entered into every phase of the life of its people—their landscapes, their temples, their gardens and, in the rural areas, their homes. It was the spare clarity of Zen.

Zen is a religion of quietude. Even words can be deemed treacherous when instead of the naked reality of existence one only grasps at a form of words. D. T. Suzuki, in his classic text on the subject, says that "Zen is not necessarily against words, but is well aware of the fact that they are always liable to detach themselves from realities and turn themselves into conceptions. And this conceptualisation is what Zen is against. . . . Zen insists on handling the thing itself and not an empty abstraction. It is for this reason that Zen neglects reading or reciting the sutras or engaging in discourse on abstract subjects." Thus study, hypothesis, analysis and synthesis are ignored in favour of the face to face encounter with what might be called reality.

In brief, Zen upholds intuition against intellect, for intuition is the more direct way of reaching out to the immediacy of experience here and now. The truth is that life reveals itself most significantly when you do not clutch at it, either with your feelings or with your questing intellect. It reveals itself most clearly when you concentrate on the contentment of doing one thing at a time. Unlike the West, where nothing is allowed just to be and to mean itself, where everything has to signify something else, Zen emphasises what is described as the 'isness' or the 'suchness' of a kettle, a branch of flowering prunus or a ray of sunshine. The courage to be right here, now and nowhere else, is precisely what it demands; eat when you eat, walk when you walk, garden when you garden, scrub when you scrub.

Perhaps the experience of the tea ceremony most beguilingly captures the serenity of spirit at the heart of the old Japanese culture. It encourages the elimination of unnecessaries, the virtues of simplicity and what has been called a 'gentleness of spirit'. Stressing as it does the merits of silence, a quiet exchange between friends and the contemplation of a few simple objects, the tea ceremony takes place in an unpretentious rustic structure whose interior is meant, says Nancy Wilson Ross, to be experienced as "the abode of vacancy". Here, as the kettle boils and the hissing steam gently fills the room's engaging silence, there is a sense of timelessness, of harmony and tranquillity conducive to the reverential spirit of the Zen sacrament. It is this atmosphere which pervaded the quiet cultures of the pre-industrial past.

But the silences we find in the tea ceremony are not unique in Japanese culture; the self-same serenity once pervaded its Noh drama, its ancient wooden temples, its calligraphy, its archery and ceramics. Most especially, the reflective, contemplative mood still pervades the dry landscape temple gardens of Kyoto. Fashioned from the most austere materials—sand and stone and in one case mosses—these gardens, designed to be a training ground for the spirit, breathe the very essence of Zen. Nothing could be more peaceful, embodying the deepest contemplative calm.

The simple directness and instantaneous perception of haiku—a highly abbreviated verse of seventeen syllables dealing with the simplest of everyday observations—is also replete with verses celebrating the wonder of everyday life, a magical sense of the intersection of the timeless and the ephemeral. Basho's famous haiku about a frog takes place in a setting so quiet that the sound of a leaping frog has the impact of a thunderclap:

> An old pond,
> A frog leaps in,
> The sound of water.

Noise, so characteristic of the casual vandalism of modernity, plays no part in the ancient Japanese mode of poetical life.

THE SILENCE OF THE CHINESE HERMITS

> The hermit escapes the human world
> and likes to sleep on mountains
> among green widely spaced vines
> where clear torrents sing harmonies.
> He steams with joy, swinging at ease through freedom,
> not stained with worldly affairs,
> heart clean as a white lotus.
> *Han Shan (translated by Tony Barnstone and Chou Ping)*

Old Chinese landscape paintings reveal, among towering mountains, waterfalls and forests, the frail outline of a roof, and on occasion a meditating figure. Some are gazing into space; their figures diminutive, the landscape extensive. In his *Road to Heaven: Encounters with Chinese Hermits*, Bill Porter presents a sympathetic account of the hermetic tradition and its contemporary manifestation. "Throughout Chinese history, there have always been people who preferred to spend their lives in the mountains, getting by on less, sleeping under thatch, wearing old clothes, working the higher slopes, not talking much, writing even less—maybe a few poems, a recipe or two. Out of touch with the times but not with the seasons, they cultivated roots of the spirit, trading flat-land dust for mountain mist. Distant and insignificant, they were the most respected men and women in the world's oldest society. . . . As far back as records go, there were always hermits in China."

Hermits were shamans and diviners, herbalists and doctors; they were adepts of the occult and could talk to heaven. The Chinese have always looked to hermits as amongst their greatest social benefactors, but after the ravages of the Cultural Revolution, did they still exist? Bill Porter set out to explore, starting in the Chungan Mountains near Sian, to find if and how far the tradition survived.

Well, it does—just. He encounters Taoist hermits, Buddhist her-mits, and intellectual hermits who prefer quiet and seclusion in order to study or write. But their numbers are fewer than in the past. Historians of the Han Dynasty (206 BC–221 AD) say there were thirteen hundred Taoist masters of note during the reign of Emperor Ming, but today there are probably fewer than a hundred and fifty Taoist monks and nuns in all of China. As one observes, "Taoism teaches us to reduce our desires and to lead quiet lives. People willing to reduce their desires or cultivate tranquillity in this modern age are very few. This is the age of desire . . . But the important thing is to learn to still your mind. Once you can do that, you can live anywhere, even in a noisy city."

"One of the mountains we visited was Tailaoshan just inside the northwest tip of Fukien Province. A Buddhist layman we met on the trail led us to a cave where an eighty-five year old monk had been living for the last fifty years. In the course of our conversation, the monk asked me who this Chairman Mao was whom I kept mentioning. He said he had moved into the cave in 1939 after the spirits of the moun-tain appeared to him in a dream and asked him to become the moun-tain's protector. He hadn't been down the mountain since then. Disciples and local villagers brought him the few things he needed. And he didn't need much: flour, cooking oil, salt, and once every five years or so a new blanket or set of robes. His practice was the name of the Buddha: Amitabha, Buddha of the Infinite."

On another occasion, Porter encounters an eighty-eight year old nun, Yuan-chao, who had taught Buddhism to many students for many years. "From my bag, I took out a sheet of calligraphy paper and asked if she would write down for me the essence of Buddhist practice. She put the paper aside, and I didn't raise the subject again. Two months later, back in Taiwan, I received the sheet of paper in the mail with four words: goodwill, compassion, joy, detachment. Her calligraphy was as clear as her mind."

Asked if he had ever felt lonely another monk replied: "No, not as long as I have the wind and the moon, the water and the mountains for my companions." And another: "If people are quiet, they can be quiet anywhere. If people aren't quiet, they won't be quiet here."

THE AGE OF NOISE

> The twentieth century is, among other things, the Age of Noise. Physical noise, mental noise, the noise of desire—we hold history's record for all of them. And no wonder; for all the resources of our almost miraculous technology have been thrown into the current assault against silence.
> *Aldous Huxley*

It was the nineteenth century's industrial revolution, with its indomitable spirit of speed, its cogs and wheels and metal, that introduced mechanical and amplified din into the factories, the railway termini, the airports, the homes and streets of the modern world. Spots of noise have always existed, but usually in the context of a silent, or relatively silent, environment. After the industrial revolution, noise began to spread out like the ripples generated by a stone thrown into a pond.

In *The Adventures of Oliver Twist* (1837–39) Charles Dickens describes Smithfield market, an oasis of noise in the relative quietness of the surrounding streets, in words of celebratory enthusiasm:

> Countrymen, butchers, drovers, hawkers, boys, thieves, idlers, and vagabonds of every low grade, were mingled together in a mass; the whistling of drovers, the barking of dogs, the bellowing and plunging of oxen, the bleating of sheep, the grunting and squealing of pigs, the cries of hawkers, the shouts, oaths, and quarrelling on all sides; the ringing of bells and roar of

voices, that issued from every public house; the crowding, pushing, driving, beating, whooping and yelling; the hideous and discordant din that resounded from every corner of the market . . . rendered it a stunning and bewildering scene, which quite confounded the senses.

But if modern Smithfield is probably no quieter—even louder—its cacophony has now become integral to the seamless clamour of the surrounding streets where noise from cars, lorries, aeroplanes, Muzak in shops or people shouting into their mobile phones is, by both day and night, incessant. Peace and quiet (and darkness) have become considerably harder to find. Everywhere the background drone, and, at night, the glow of electric light. Life without them has become not only undesirable, but impossible to find. I fear that many people would now feel existentially uncomfortable in deep silence, deep peace and darkness. Likewise they would find it unbearable without the comfort of manufactured *stuff*.

Yet for millions of years people found life not merely tolerable but enjoyable without the gadgetry and conveniences of modern life. The great seventeenth-century painter Vermeer of Delft (1632–75) is a case in point, but not an entirely exceptional one. His rare work, renowned for its celebration of domestic scenes of order and tranquillity, speaks of stillness, serenity, calm; it belongs to a tradition of looking at things, a certain tenderness and smallness of mind that avoids the magnificent, the infinite and eternal but values the precious treasures and inexhaustible riches of everday life. But the interiors of the houses he paints were never equipped with any labour-saving devices, or even with electricity. Nonetheless, apart from human intercourse they were always blessedly quiet: no telephones demanding attention, no commercials on the television, no computer games, no sound of passing machinery in the road outside—only quietness, such as the quietness of a flute by still water, or that of rain on a window pane. To stand before the 'Woman Pouring Milk' in the Rijksmuseum in Amsterdam, to notice how the light bathes the room's whitewashed wall, to admire the dairymaid, her attention solely focused on the work in hand, to contemplate the hanging wicker bread basket, is to comprehend how deeply silence dominated the life of the past. No less serene is the work of the other Dutch painters of Vermeer's time: Pieter de Hooch and Pieter Saenredam, in whose work the realm of silence is no less absolute; not a whisper or a falling leaf can be heard in the rooms and church interiors they painted. Only "a peace that passeth all understanding".

Another contemporary figure, the Englishman Izaak Walton (1593–1683), went so far as to inscribe the words "Study to be Quiet" on the title page of the work by which he is most celebrated, *The Compleat Angler* of 1653. Interestingly, Walton later published a biography of the poet divine, George Herbert (1593–1633), whose life and work are impregnated by the most beautiful stillness.

In the seventeenth century, England was peculiarly rich, if not in mystics, at any rate in mystically minded men. These include George Fox (1624–1691), who taught his Quakers to wait upon God in a silence that was reminiscent of the *via negativa* of the mediaeval philosophers, and the poets John Donne (1572–1631) and Thomas Vaughan (1621–1695), whose work is no less embedded with stillness.

CHAPTER TWO

Staying Quietly in One's Room

*The sole cause of man's unhappiness is that
he does not know how to stay quietly in his room.*

BLAISE PASCAL.

*You don't need to leave your room. Remain sitting
at your table and listen. Don't even listen, simply wait.
Don't even wait, be quite still and solitary.
The world will freely offer itself to you to be unmasked.*

FRANZ KAFKA

Pascal's and Kafka's observations run contrary to the modern insistence that true happiness is to be found in vigorous physical action—travel, skiing, water sports, athletics, even shopping—rather than such contemplative pursuits as reading, painting and fishing. Nonetheless, some of the most deeply contented people have experienced lives characterised by silence and peacefulness—many monks and nuns, philosophers and scholars, mystics and gardeners, writers and creative artists; farmers, mothers and nurses, too.

For them, instead of the stimulation that characterises so much modern life, the quietude of the study or studio, the stillness of the place of prayer, the calm of the dairy, the silence of the field, the dedication to a noble cause, provide the unruffled context for a life of peace. For peace has to be chosen and worked for, and it comes, as Yeats wrote in *The Lake Island of Innisfree*, "dropping slow".

> I will arise and go now, and go to Innisfree
> And a small cabin build there, of clay and wattle made;
> Nine bean rows will I have there, a hive for the honeybee,
> And live alone in the bee-loud glade.
> And I shall have some peace there, for peace comes dropping slow;
> Dropping from the veils of the morning to where the cricket sings;
> There midnight's all a-glimmer, and noon a purple glow
> And evening full of the linnet's wings.
> I will arise and go now, for always night and day
> I hear lake water lapping with low sounds by the shore;
> While I stand on the roadway, or on the pavements gray,
> I hear it in the deep heart's core.

HILDEGARD OF BINGEN

There is no creation that does not have a radiance. Be it greenness or seed, blossom or beauty, it could not be creation without it—the world is living, being, spirit, all verdant greening, all creativity. All creation awakened, called, by the resounding melody, God's invocation of the word.
Hildegard of Bingen

By her works, Hildegard de Bingen (1098–1179) was one of the most remarkable people to have ever lived. Besides being the abbess of a large and prosperous Benedictine abbey, she was a prominent preacher, doctor, scientist, and artist. She was also a poet and composer, writing nine books on theology, medicine, science, and physiology, as well as seventy poems. Among her many literary works Hildegard produced two books of natural history and medicine and a morality play, the *Ordu virtutum*, which predates all other works in that genre by some hundred years.

After the age of forty, when she began to have visions, with the help of the monk Volmar and the nun Richardis she began to record these visions in her first major visionary work, *Scivitas* [Know the Ways], which occupied her between 1141 and 1151. The most important manuscript of this book, completed in c.1165, contains a series of painted miniatures which depict the visions she experienced and described. These are amongst the most remarkable images of European art. In her lifetime, Hildegard was to complete two other books of visions. In addition she wrote the stories of saints' lives and nearly seventy-seven vocal compositions which contain some of the finest songs to be written in the Middle Ages (see page 120).

Although born in a world in turmoil and actively participating in its religious and secular affairs, Hildegard's life and work were imbued with a fathomless stillness. That stillness is to be heard in her musical compositions suffused by a luminous, unearthly beauty. "Search out the house of your heart," she advises, and she herself does. I imagine her in the abbey's church, singing alongside her sisters; in the scriptorium dictating letters to her secretary, the young monk, Volmar; in her simple, whitewashed cell, composing music, spinning, reading; I can hear her heavy clothes swishing the ground as she moves from room to room; I can sense the magnetism and energy of this extraordinary woman for whom the wonder of creation was never an esoteric thing but immediately and perpetually visible.

Born to the noble family of Hildebert of Gut Bermersheim near Alzey in Rhinehessen (now in west Germany), Hildegard exhibited exceptional gifts as a young girl. When she had scarcely learned to speak, she sought to convey to those around her something of the remarkable visionary life which was intrinsic to her nature.

At the age of eight, her spiritual training was assumed by the abbess of the nearby cloister, Jutta von Spaanheim. There she was instructed in the rules of the Benedictine Order, the liturgy, and the various liberal arts. She would have learnt to pray the Psalter in Latin and have heard, and later taken part in, the cycle of prayer and chanting which comprises the monastic life. When Hildegard was fifteen she took the habit of a Benedictine nun, and when Jutta died in 1136, was elected as leader of her community.

Throughout her life Hildegard was continually afflicted by illness. In 1141, she tells us, this receded and gave way to a series of religious visions: she saw tongues of flame descend from heavens and settle upon her. Thereafter she devoted herself to a life of intense and passionate creativity. She was deeply aware of the importance of creativity, which she urged upon all people, declaring that we are indeed "co-creators with God." She urged all people to fly since "we all have wings to fly", and to shout with joy simply because we are created.

In his book *Illuminations of Hildegard de Bingen*, Matthew Fox has drawn attention to a concept peculiar to Hildegard as a theologian— her use of the word *viriditas* or greening power. She talks of "the exquisite greening of trees and grasses", of "earth's lush greening". She says that all of creation, and humanity in particular, is "showered with greening refreshment, the vitality to bear fruit". "In the beginning," she relates, "all creatures were green and vital; they flourished among flowers." Such a feeling for earth's ancient sweetness, its capacity for renewal, its sense of, as Gerard Manley Hopkins wrote, "the dearest freshness deep down things", its germinating force, can be seen as a synonym for the blessings of fruitfulness or creativity.

Yet for all her work as an artist, writer and composer, which gave expression to her joy in and about existence, for all her responsibilities as the mother and leader of her community to whom she devoted herself in the spirit of love, Hildegard never turned her back on her world. She was seriously engaged in politics and diplomacy, and her friendship and advice were sought by popes, kings, archbishops, abbots and abbesses, with whom she corresponded voluminously. These included letters to such celebrities as Fredrich Barbarossa and Bernard de Clairvaux.

Although highly educated in the intellectual traditions of her time, Hildegard presented herself above all as a person operating not through her own knowledge but as the *instrumentum* of God's will. "The words I speak come from no human mouth; I saw and heard them in visions sent to me." These then were visions which came to her in the silences of her convent, the silences of her study, the silences which pervaded every aspect of her exceptionally energetic life. Thus solitude, poverty, obedience and prayer disposed her soul for the mysterious work of creation in which she excelled.

Like the nun and playwright Hroswitha of Gandersheim (c.930–c.990) and the English mystic Julian of Norwich (c.1343–died after 1413), Hildegard de Bingen wrote in simple, homely style. But like so many others whose core of being is rooted in silence, she was not only an artist and a poet but an actor on the stage of life. All records of mysticism in the West are also the records of supreme human activity. Not only of 'wrestlers of the spirit' but also of great organisers: St Teresa, St John of the Cross, St Francis of Assisi, St Ignatius Loyola, Meister Eckhart, George Fox, St Bernard, St Catherine of Siena and Saint Joan of Arc are amongst the most inspiring examples. The paradoxical 'quiet' of the contemplative is but the outward stillness essential to inward and to outer work.

Hildegard died at the age of 81 years in 1179.

RYOKAN

> I've never bothered about getting ahead
> But just gone leisurely along letting things take their way.
> In my bag are three measures of rice
> A bundle of firewood sits by the hearth
> Who cares about delusion and enlightenment?
> What use is there in fame and fortune?
> In my hut I listen to the evening rain
> And stretch my legs without a care in the world.

Like Hildegard, the poet-monk Taigu Ryokan (1758–1831) was a contemplative and an artist. One of the most popular figures in Japanese Buddhist history, he too is a heart-warming example of a person who lived his life intensely, unselfconsciously, and without the least trace of pretension. In contrast to the Zen masters of his time who presided over large monasteries, he followed the life of a penniless monk, spent in obscurity in Japan's snow country, meditating, playing with children and writing poems that vividly describe his world. He lived by begging in local villages and towns, beloved by all, celebrated for his warmth and wisdom, and legendary for his *naïveté*, which made him the butt of countless practical jokes. Today he is the subject of numerous books—some 3,500 by 1985.

Although Ryokan's thatched hermitage was sited deep in the mountains, he often visited the neighbouring villages to play with the children, drink saké with the farmers, or visit his friends. He slept when he wanted to, drank freely, and joined in the dancing parties held in the summer. Although he acquired his simple means by mendicancy, whenever he had anything extra he gave it away. Like St Francis, his life radiated purity and joy.

Despite his religious and artistic sophistication (he excelled in poetry, calligraphy and scriptural studies), Ryokan liked to refer to himself as a "Great Fool". In his book of translations of some of his poetry, John Stevens relates two delightful stories about his life. The first tells how Ryokan talked for several hours to a visitor to the hermitage. As evening drew in, Ryokan suggested that some saké might help their conviviality, and it was agreed that he should go and fetch reinforcements. "The friend waited and waited, but Ryokan did not return. When Hosai could stand it no longer, he went out to find him. To his astonishment, he saw the monk about a hundred yards from the hermitage, sitting under a pine tree, gazing dreamily at a full moon. 'Ryokan! Where have you been? I've been waiting for you for more than three hours! I thought something terrible had happened to you!', he shouted. 'Hosai-san! You have come just in time. Isn't the moon splendid?', Ryokan enthused."

The other story is no less innocuously childlike. "One spring afternoon, Ryokan noticed three bamboo shoots growing under his veranda. Bamboo grows rapidly, and soon the shoots were pressing against the bottom of the veranda. Ryokan was quite anxious, for he did not like anything to suffer, even plants. He cut three holes in the floor and then told the bamboo shoots not to worry; he would cut a hole in the roof if necessary. He was happy again."

Far from being highly crafted and refined, Ryokan's poems are as spontaneous and direct as his life: simple and pure. Here is one of them:

> Truly, I love this life of seclusion.
> Carrying my staff, I walk towards a friend's cottage.
> The trees in his garden, soaked by the evening rain,
> Reflect the cool, clear autumnal sky.
> The owner's dog comes to meet me;
> Chrysanthemums bloom along the fence,
> These people have the same spirit as the ancients;
> An earthen wall marks their separation from the world,
> In the house volumes of poetry are piled on the floor.
> Abandoning worldliness, I often come to this tranquil place—
> The spirit here is the spirit of Zen.

EMILY DICKINSON

> How happy is the little Stone
> That rambles in the Road alone,
> And doesn't care about Careers
> And Exigencies never fears—
> Whose Coat of elemental Brown
> A passing Universe put on,
> And independent as the Sun
> Associates or glows alone,
> Fulfilling absolute Decree
> In casual simplicity—

Emily Dickinson (1830–1886) was also a poet of silence and something of a recluse. Born into a conventional, comfortable family in the provincial town of Amherst, Massachusetts, where her family had long been associated with the Calvinistically inclined Church, and her father was President of Amherst College, she hardly ever left the town or her parents' house throughout her life. By the time she was thirty she had stopped going to services in her church. Soon she did not leave the house at all. She stayed in, listening to her inner moods and conversing with herself, in verse, about what she heard there. By her fortieth year she was dressing solely in white and seeing only a few of the callers who came to the homestead. Over time, she withdrew even further into herself and her environment: first into the house and garden, then into the house, then simply and solely into her room. Her choice of solitude was as compulsive as that of a contemplative nun, yet she was too original to be considered a conventionally religious person. "My family," she wrote, "are Religious, except me, and address an Eclipse, every morning, whom they call their Father." She herself was independent of man or God: "You ask of my Companions. Hills, sir and the Sundown, and a Dog as large as myself, that my Father bought me. They are better than Beings, because they Know, but do not tell; and the Noise in the Pool at Noon excels my piano."

Emily Dickinson had been writing poems since her adolescence; but suddenly, in her early thirties, she began to write as if possessed. In her thirty-second year she wrote 366 poems alone. Only a handful were published in her lifetime. For years, thousands of these ambiguous, playful, urgently beautiful works lay unread in a box in the family home; it was not until 1890, four years after her death (and two years after Walt Whitman's), that they began to be known.

Her 1,175 poems reveal a passionate, witty woman, and a scrupulous craftswoman who made an art not only of her poetry but also of her correspondence and her life. Although several of her poems deal with God, Dickinson remained a sceptic.

Her poetry is the innocent utterance of one for whom solitude fostered the richness of her soul's interior abundance. It gives to her writing a most vivid sense of the eternal otherness which, she believed, lies in wait for us all. In her poems about the soul's choice, about moments of fear or glory or vision, she conveys her sense of the challenge and mystery generated by experience—an experience gleaned in solitude in her quiet bedroom.

HENRY DAVID THOREAU

> Our inventions are wont to be pretty toys, which distract our attention from serious things. They are but improved means to an unimproved end, an end which it was already but too easy to arrive at . . .
> *Henry David Thoreau*

Emily Dickinson's contemporary, also a poet, is more celebrated for his account of his two or so years solitary stay in a cabin beside Walden Pond, close to Concord, Massachusetts. Henry David Thoreau (1817–62) was quite a sociable hermit, saying that he had three chairs in his house: one for solitude, two for friendship, three for society. But by choice he mostly lived by himself. In *Walden; or Life in the Woods*, (published in 1854), which combines personal narrative with scientific observation, moral philosophy, spiritual meditation and ruminations about politics and economics, he provides us with an explanation of why he came to seek so much solitude:

> I went to the woods because I wished to live deliberately, to front only the essential facts of life, to see if I could not learn what I'd to teach, and not, when I came to die, discover that I had not lived. . . . I wanted to live deep and suck out all the marrow of life, to live so sturdily and Spartan-like as to put to rout all that was not life, to cut the broad swath and shave close, to drive life into a corner, and reduce it to its lowest terms, and if it were sublime, to know it by experience.

Thoreau liked building, and had done some work on a new house for his parents not far away. He began by cutting down some of the white pines, then he bought an abandoned shanty for its well-weathered boards, and set to work. He also cleared two acres of brambles for a vegetable garden, and passed his time in carpentry, gardening and writing. His cabin was simple (ten by fifteen feet of living space in the main rooms, plus a loft, a tiny garret and potato cellar) and simply furnished; he writes that he was proud of the fact that his mirror was no bigger than a penny postcard.

Thoreau shows (as so many others have done before and since) that it is only when the restless mind has been stilled that we can truly encounter what is unfolding before us. This unfolding he lived from hour to hour and day to day. It was a manifestation expressed in a couplet originally scribbled down in his Journal:

> My life has been the poem I would have writ,
> But I could not both live and utter it.

Walden is filled with fierce and meticulous observations of the world he saw around him—its birds, its light, its sounds, the magical beauty of the few square miles of unfrequented forest in which he lived. "What is a course of history or philosophy or poetry," he writes, "no matter how well selected, or the best society, or the most admirable routine of life, compared with the discipline of looking always at what is to be seen?" He also wrote: "We are surrounded by a rich and fertile mystery. May we not probe it, pry into it, employ ourselves a little—a little?"

> Sometimes, in a summer morning, having taken my accustomed bath, I sat in my sunny doorway from sunrise till noon, rapt in a reverie, amidst the pines and hickories and sumachs, in undisturbed solitude and stillness, while the birds sang around or flitted noiseless through the house, until the sun falling in at my west window, or the noise of some travellers wagon on the distant highway, I was reminded of the lapse of time. I grew in those seasons like corn in the night . . .

PAUL CEZANNE

> Work regardless of anyone and achieve mastery. That should be the artist's goal.
> *Paul Cézanne*

Another artist whose work, like Thoreau's, arises out of a ground of calm and silence, and to which in turn he was to give one of its most monumental expressions, is the French painter, probably the greatest of recent times, Paul Cézanne (1839–1906).

Cézanne lived in seclusion in a quiet and rather old-fashioned part of France, Aix-en-Provence, where he was born in 1839. He lived the quiet life; perhaps no other nineteenth century painter has less to tell us about the dramas of that tumultuous century. His pictures tell no stories; they are not self-expressive; they make no concessions to haste. As a painter Cézanne worked with absolute dedication and with extreme patience and slowness, vehemently but with an agonising care. One of the people he painted, the dealer Ambroise Vollard, wrote of his experience:

> I had been told that Cézanne made a slave of his models. I proved it to my own satisfaction from sad experience. From the moment he put down the first brushstroke until the end of the sitting, he treated the model like a simple still life. He loved to paint portraits. 'The goal of all art,' he would say, 'is the human face.' If he did not paint it more often, the reason lay in the difficulty of procuring models who were as tractable as me. Consequently, after painting himself and his wife many times, and also a few obliging friends . . . he resorted to painting apples, and even more frequently flowers—flowers did not decay: he used paper ones. But 'even they, confound 'em! faded in the long run' . . .
>
> After 115 sittings, Cézanne abandoned my portrait to return to Aix. 'The front of the shirt is not bad'—such were his last words on parting. He made me leave the clothes in which I posed at the studio, expecting, when he returned to Paris, to paint in the two white spots on the hands, and then, of course, to work over certain parts. 'I hope to have made some progress by that time. You understand, Monsieur Vollard, the contour keeps slipping away from me!' But he had not counted on the moths, 'the little wretches!' which devoured my clothes in short order . . .

Cézanne's art is not like that of other painters; its tautness and muscularity, its monumental design and saturated colour (of a purity hardly ever surpassed), was the result of an impersonal but sustained contemplation of the things of this world: some apples and oranges on a table, a crumpled linen napkin, the face of his wife and the landscape around Aix which he traversed and observed on a daily basis for over four decades. It has been said of the painter that he did not paint "Look at me," but "Here it is."

His practice did not begin with a belief in a transcendent reality but with fidelity to observed facts, to things as they are, aware and alert in the present moment. "Lucidity before nature" was one of the favourite phrases of this painter, on whom one can meditate endlessly as on the life and works of a saint. Yet the poet Rainer Maria Rilke's attraction to Cézanne's works was not primarily aesthetic; for him there was a presence in them of the artist's nearness to God, and it was this that moved him.

Certainly, no less than lucidity, silence is a pervasive characteristic of his work. In his last years Cézanne, always a solitary, went out of his way to find themes of a grandiose solitude. He painted the secluded shadowy interiors of the local woods, rocky ledges, unused quarries and ruined buildings. It is the world of a hermit, in which ideas of death are never far away. Returning to the studio, he delighted in painting skulls upon the table where he had recently piled ensembles of oranges and onions.

Today, his studio outside Aix on the Chemin des Lauves is open to the interested visitor; the table with its scalloped apron front, the blue ginger pot, the green olive jar, various containers and crockery—the common place objects Cézanne immortalised in his work—are still on display. It is empty; a fly buzzes against a window pane. The sunshine beats on the view beyond the open door. What concentration of silence pervades this space!

GIORGIO MORANDI

Another painter, the Italian Giorgio Morandi, was if anything even more solitary, more unhurried, more austere than Cézanne, whose work he greatly loved. Morandi was born in Bologna in 1890, lived in that city all his life and died there in 1964. He never joined, as many others did, any movement; he travelled nowhere, did a little teaching, and spent the last forty-five years of his life in two slightly musty flats which he shared with his three sisters. Indeed, one of the few upheavals of his life was when the four of them left their birth-place at via Fondazza 34 in Bologna and moved next door, to number 36. But even in the flats, Morandi didn't go far since he slept in his studio, on a narrow iron bed. Very few, not even his sisters, were admitted to the studio, where over the years dust settled on the bottles, bowls, vases and other simple objects that he contemplated, drew and painted continuously.

He treated these with an exceptional tenderness, never hurrying, absorbed by the wisdom of slowness. "It takes me weeks to make up my mind which groups of bottles will go well with a particular tablecloth," he said. "Then it takes me weeks of thinking about the bottles themselves, and yet often I still go wrong with the spaces. Perhaps I work too fast?" For his contemporary, the French painter Georges Braque, there could be only one answer to that question. He measured his work not in weeks but years.

"To meditate," says the Buddhist scholar Stephen Batchelor, "is to probe with intense sensitivity each glimmer of colour, each cadence of sound." For hour after hour, day after day, for some fifty years, Morandi did no more. It is no surprise that one critic nicknamed him *Il monaco*, "the monk".

"Throughout his career," writes Robert Hughes, "Italian culture buzzed with manifestos, claims and counter claims. Before World War I, the Futurists tried to marshal art into a relentless machine-age spectacle. In the twenties and thirties, Mussolini and his cultural gang strove to co-opt Italian modernism into Fascist propaganda—dynamism, simplification. By the late forties and fifties, so-called realism (especially in Bologna, which took pride in its worker traditions) was trying, amid clouds of Stalinist rhetoric, to become the house style of Italian art. All through this, Morandi stayed where he was, looking at his plain table of dusty bottles."

With his Franciscan devotion to these unpretentious things—the curvature of the shoulder of a vase, the quivering outline of a box, a juxtaposition of the tones of a shadow and the wall upon which it falls—he raised his still lives to the kind of glory that Christ saw in the lilies of the field. "We need nothing but open eyes, to be ravished," said the seventeenth-century English mystic Thomas Traherne.

To be ravished in this way is to be open, as Morandi always was, to the miracle of life—its shapes, colours, tones, textures and spaces. He confessed that the surest way of astonishing oneself is to stare fixedly at the same object, which will miraculously seem as though we have never seen it before. Morandi had discovered that everything is a mystery, ourselves and the simplest things.

HARLAN HUBBARD

Harlan Hubbard (1900–1986), an American painter, writer and small-holder, and his wife Anna shared something of Morandi's delight for the humblest, simplest things. Early in his life he saw that our present society could not deliver on its promises of human improvement. In response he and his wife set themselves apart from industrial values, to live alone in the silences and truthfulness of a life of self-sufficiency. Their existence became a public demonstration that a life of self-reliant wholeness was economically feasible, physically practicable, and spiritually desirable.

By 1929, when he began keeping a journal, his differences from the dominant assumptions of his times were well established. In 1944, he and Anna built with their own hands a shantyboat on which they voyaged down the Ohio and Mississippi rivers, ending in the Louisiana bayous in 1951. From 1952 until their deaths, they lived in a house they built themselves at Payne Hollow beside the Ohio River. Here they cut firewood, tended a herd of goats, fished, grew vegetables, welcomed friends, painted, made music and lived with an unhurried dignity.

In *Shantyboat: A River Way of Life* he wrote about their aims:

> I had no theories to prove. I merely wanted to try living by my own hands, independently as far as possible from a system of division of labour in which the participant loses most of the pleasure of making and growing things for himself. I wanted to bring in my own fuel and smell its sweet smell as it burned in the hearth I had made. I wanted to grow my own food, or forage after it. In short I wanted to do as much as I could for myself, because I had already realised from partial experience the inexpressible joy of so doing.

In a moving passage in his book in celebration of their lives, their friend the American poet and novelist Wendell Berry writes about their life together:

> Their common effort to make a life 'in harmony with the landscape' involved the making of a harmony between their own somewhat divergent characters. Their marriage is best understood, perhaps, as a harmony between seemingly opposite themes of domesticity and wilderness. Anna's was clearly a refining

and domesticating influence. She was a home maker in the fullest, finest sense of the term; she loved the order, elegance and dignity, but his approach to the world was radically unlike hers. Throughout his life one of Harlan's strongest and most characteristic impulses was towards what he called wilderness, by which he seems not to have meant necessarily the pristine natural settings to which that word is often applied, for he did not seek out such places, but rather the unmediated presence of the earth itself, wherever and however it might be encountered. Harlan loved the river and the hills, he loved the weather, he loved to go out into the weather. He loved the night sky and 'the unalloyed darkness of night'. He loved all his returning to what he called 'the earth' from 'the world' of modern urbanisation and machinery.

THOMAS MERTON

Let me seek, then, the gift of silence, and poverty, and solitude, where everything I touch is turned into prayer: where the sky is my prayer, the birds are my prayer, the wind in the trees are my prayer, for God is all in all.
Thomas Merton

The silence of the forest, the peace of the early morning wind moving the branches of the trees, the solitude and isolation of the house of God, these are good because it is in silence, and not in commotion, in solitude and not in crowds, that God best likes to reveal Himself most intimately to men.
Thomas Merton

My final choice of a person rooted in silence but far from silent, was a contemporary of the Hubbards, Thomas Merton (1915–1968), a monk of the Cistercian Order of Strict Observance, and what might now be described as an 'engaged' Christian. He lived in a hermitage in Louisville, where he wrote the vast majority of his prodigious output—some sixty titles are currently in print in English. His early works were strictly spiritual, but in the early 1960s his writings tended towards social criticism. Merton was the author of many books, including *The Seven Story Mountain* (1948), *Seeds of Contemplation*, *Wisdom of the Desert*, *The Silent Life* and *Contemplation in a World of Action*, and also a photographer. His growing interest in Eastern religions led him to attend a conference in Bangkok, where he died in 1968, aged only 53.

In the world of sixties America, Merton helped many to develop a theology of resistance: to the Vietnam war, to structural racism, to the nuclear threat, to an increasingly repressive and authoritarian culture. He was not afraid to condemn the realities of American life and the forces shaping and distorting the modern world. For example, he recognised and warned against the new religious Right, a phenomenon which became a political reality in 1979 with the birth of the Moral Majority, and the forces which led to the Reagan victory, and more recently to the election and re-election of George Bush. In 1964 Merton wrote of "the mystique of American Christian Rightism, a mystique of violence, of apocalyptic threats, of hatred and of judgement", rooted in the "conviction that the great evil in the world today can be identified in Communism, and that to be a Christian is simply to be anti-Communist." It was twenty years later that President Reagan described Soviet Communism as the "focus of evil in the modern world"; now it seems (according to President Bush, another Christian), Iran, North Korea and Iraq present a new "axis of evil".

Merton was a contemplative monk, and yet as his life and writings show, his grasp of the realities of American culture and of the signs of his times was often greater than that of many politicians, commentators and diplomats, supposedly more conversant with the realities of worldly affairs. With his contemplative insight, he was able to observe the delusions of government and a self-serving establishment religion. He wrote often of the "unmasking of illusion" as a central prophetic task. Like William Blake, another figure to choose silence, creativity and solitude rather than fame and worldly influence, Thomas Merton was an authentic prophet for his age.

Such people are not alone in understanding the value of dedication, attentive contemplation, creativity and silence. I think of the Catalan architect Antoni Gaudí,[2] the sculptor Constantin Brancusi, the painter Georges Braque, and the Italian composer Luigi Nono (on whose Venetian house a plaque reads 'Master of sound and silence'). Some, like Emily Dickinson, Ryokan and Georgio Morandi, have elected to live in virtual solitude; others, like Thoreau, Cézanne and Harlan Hubbard, have not only chosen to celebrate the goodness and beauty of the earth but to make the least impact upon it; yet others, like Hildegard and Merton, have sought to bear witness to the importance of healing and balance in the affairs of the world.

Yet none expressed the least desire for celebrity, wealth or 'success' as it is currently understood. Movements of any stripe, political, social or cultural, were also not for them. Any 'ism' was too doctrinaire, too programmatic, too collective. From first to last, each was his or her own person. All were rooted to a well-loved place: Hildegard to her cloister at Disibodenberg, Ryokan to his hermitage on Mount Kugami (his home for some twenty-six years), Emily Dickinson to her parents' house in Amherst, Thoreau to Concord, Cézanne to a small area round Aix-en-Provence, Morandi to Bologna, Hubbard to Payne Hollow, and Merton to his hermitage in the grounds of the Abbey of Gethsemani at Trappist, Kentucky. All spoke of the importance of silence and solitude as the conducive ground for creativity and a focused awareness of the miracle of existence.

Such lives can be dismissed as inconsequential only by those who cannot see their value to modern culture. By poverty of means, by love and creative action, they have contributed an example for others to fol-low. Future generations without our present resources, with land abused and cities characterised by size and ugliness, suffering, too, the devastating consequences of global warming, may look to them for guidance towards the salvation of their world.

CHAPTER THREE

The Enemies of Silence

The enemies of silence are twofold. First there are the external interruptions to one's peace of mind. Consider the increasing difficulty of finding tranquillity anywhere. In a city, a small town, even a village, it is becoming virtually impossible: everywhere there is noise, unceasing disturbance even throughout the night. Perhaps a park may offer a modicum of solace, but it is only relative; the hum of traffic is insistent, people are hurrying past and shouting into their mobile phones. An aeroplane rumbles overhead. Nor is the deep countryside always an improvement: helicopters, planes, lorries, buggies, tractors and combine harvesters continuously invade its peace. The remote Devon parish on the edge of Dartmoor where Robert Herrick held a living now drums with the traffic on the A30 passing a few feet from its ancient church. The contrast between the quiet lyricism of Herrick's verse and the ceaseless drone of rushing vehicles demonstrates only too vividly the silence and the peace of mind that has been lost.

Another poet, suffering the visit of "a man on business from Porlock", was famously interrupted in his writing of 'Kubla Khan'. It was October 1797, and Coleridge was staying in a solitary farmhouse (probably Ash Farm at the head of Culbone Combe) in a remote area above the cliffs between Porlock Bay and Lynton; disastrous as this interruption may have been, it was an isolated event. For us distraction has become a more permanent condition of our daily life: there are countless ways in which we can be—and are—interrupted. Distraction is now so familiar that it enjoys something of the permanency of a way of life in itself.

If the first enemy of silence comes from outside, the second and more insidious is internal; it is the Trojan horse we have invited into our own lives. As an enemy, this one doesn't carry a squadron of armed men intent on overtaking a besieged city, but something no less secretive and lethal: it is the baggage of ideas, beliefs and assumptions we carry around in our minds.

Of course, some of these may be more conducive to the spirit of concentration than others. This is self-evidently true of the underlying philosophy in a monastic setting, where everything has been chosen to inculcate a peaceful, meditative stillness. The pace of life is slow; the reading calculated to dispose the soul for its mysterious destiny in God; the plainchant is no less reverential. Compared with the hatred and violence inherent in the 'philosophy' of National Socialism (as revealed in

Leni Riefenstahl's film of the 1934 Nuremberg rally, *Triumph of the Will*), the atmosphere of the monastery is deeply tranquil.

In his fascinating book *Extraordinary Popular Delusions and the Madness of Crowds*, Charles Mackay documents a catalogue of beliefs that have led Europeans astray: the South Sea Bubble, witch mania, fortune telling, the Crusades, even tulipomania, each of which in turn have befuddled the minds of our ancestors. But, because it was published well before the twentieth century (in 1841) more recent ideologies were not mentioned. These include all the recent major political ideologies, in which the spirit of silence was (and is) completely absent: National Socialism, Bolshevism, Maoism and the ideas of Pol Pot and Sayyid Qutb (whose 1964 book *Sign Posts on the Way* inspired the jihad movement).

To describe the grip of ideas on the human mind, William Blake employed an instructive phrase. He called them "mind-forged manacles", and such, I believe, they are: imprisoning mental handcuffs from which, once fastened, there is little chance of an easy escape. Well, perhaps that's not strictly true. Once an idea has begun to lose its grip, a conscious determination to consider it can relax the hold of its oppressive blinkers. Then silence is free to make its contribution: to return us to a state of tranquillity and peace; to erase the fever and the inner turmoil of a "mind-forged manacle".

But if such faiths as Bolshevism and National Socialism had the power to move millions to take decisive and, as they saw it, self-sacrificial action, there is another belief, Modernism, which even now enjoys a pervasive hold over billions of people not only in Europe, but in China, India, and parts of the Middle East. It is the dream of what Erich Fromm called "the Great Promise of Unlimited Progress". That is to say, "the promise of domination of nature, of material abundance, of the greatest happiness for the greatest number, and of unimpeded personal freedom."

This is a belief system so ubiquitous, so unquestioned, that we are largely ignorant of its effect upon us. Yet, like the German schoolchildren indoctrinated by Nazism in the years before the last European war, we have been so conditioned to accept the premises of modernism that we do so without questioning them. These include, among other beliefs, the idea that the world exclusively exists for the purpose of serving human needs, that money and possessions enhance our happiness, that speed is important, and that schooling is an essential preparation for life.

COMPULSORY SCHOOLING

> "Now what I want is, Facts. Teach these boys and girls nothing but Facts.
> Facts alone are wanted in life. Plant nothing else, and root out everything
> else. You can only form the minds of reasoning animals on Facts; nothing else
> will ever be of any service to them."
> *Charles Dickens (Hard Times)*

Our greatest conditioning experience takes place, I suggest, during our
years at school. It is then that we absorb the ideas, the assumptions and
patterns of behaviour that define Modernism, a system of belief at variance with the one I am proposing in this book.

Compulsory 'education' between the ages of five and thirteen has a
long history, having been introduced in 1880. W. E. Forster, the MP
behind the education reforms, gave the reasons for them in a speech in
Parliament:

> "We must not delay . . . Upon the speedy provision of elementary education
> depends our industrial prosperity."

Thus the newly established industrial system was to be provided with an
army of foot soldiers trained to count, to write and to administer the factories and communications system. Today the aim of 'education' remains
primarily unchanged. It gives the individual the knowledge he or she
needs to function efficiently in an industrialised civilisation, to form his
or her character into the mould which is needed: ambitious and compet-
itive, yet co-operative within certain limits and, as Erich Fromm suggests,
"friendly, yet not deeply attached to anybody or anything".

There can be little doubt that, with fortune on one's side, those
years can be beneficial. I myself disliked the school I was obliged to
attend, but there was a teacher, the art master, who opened my eyes to a
world of beauty which I would not have otherwise encountered.

Of course, my experience was not unique. There have always been
exceptional teachers and exceptional schools fostering exceptional
strengths and values. Yet the State's educational system has not been
designed for personal development; it has been designed to discourage
any serious semblance of critical thought and, in spite of its rhetoric to

the contrary, any commitment to spiritual development, any adventure of the imagination, any condemnation of violence, any ideal of local self-sufficiency and the least taint of radicalism. The feminine principle—the loving, caring, nourishing nature of the feminine consciousness—is also prominently absent.

No less disastrously, it does nothing to instil a sense of our oneness with nature—a procedure upon which the elders of the vernacular societies, such as the Indians of the North American continent, always placed special emphasis. In its classic form, the boy of thirteen to fifteen preparing for a vision quest would consult a shaman, or similar religious figure, and then go for three or four days into some remote area where he would be alone, without food, without weapons, without belongings, directly confronting—and expecting to commune with—the forces of nature. This crucial rite of passage, a ceremony of adolescent purgation, invariably encouraged a deep sense of rootedness with the earth. Such reverence, and the respect for contemplative silence which it instilled, is completely lacking from the curriculum of most contemporary schools.

The majority of Western children who have undergone, say, ten or more years in such schools, are very different from the native adolescents whom I have described. The majority of them do not possess the power to provide themselves with anything but money, and only rarely make anything that they have produced for themselves. The children of this process grow into the adults who, to borrow the title of a short story by the novelist H. G. Wells, become the inhabitants of *The Country of the Blind* (1911): virtual automatons, whose tastes, opinions and preferences can be manipulated by the corporate monoculture.

In this context it is important to remember to protect our independence, and to have the confidence to express our native creativity. To be aware that our beliefs, our dreams and opinions, have no need to be other people's second-hand notions. It is important to remember the value of thinking for oneself, which is best done in silence.

THE EXAGGERATED IMPORTANCE OF MONEY AND THE MYTH OF CONSUMPTION

The world is too much with us; late and soon,
Getting and spending, we lay waste our powers;
Little we see in Nature that is ours;
We have given our hearts away, a sordid boon.
This Sea that bares her bosom to the moon,
The winds that will be howling at all hours,
And are up-gathered now like sleeping flowers,
For this, for everything, we are out of tune;
It moves us not...
William Wordsworth

To be clever enough to get all that money, one must be stupid enough to want it.
G. K. Chesterton

Good examination results seem to be the main purpose of schooling. They are seen as the first step on the ladder of a 'successful career', measured not by its value to the individual or society, but usually defined in terms of its earning capacity. To have 'arrived' does not mean the satisfaction of a fulfilled potential or of doing valuable social work; it means the enjoyment of wealth, leisure and status.

The widespread assumption that money is the supreme measure of achievement and happiness holds millions in its thrall. Caring for others, creative achievement, disinterested altruism, virtuous behaviour—these are still valued, but to a lesser extent than luxury and leisure, however acquired.

Nonetheless, there is only rather feeble evidence that great wealth leads to great happiness; there are too many melancholy millionaires with time on their hands for that to be so. Yet the myth persists that money brings not only pleasure but unequivocal happiness. Gandhi even prophesied that "the incessant search for material comforts and their multiplication is such an evil, and I make bold to add that the Europeans themselves will have to remodel their outlook if they are not to perish under the weight of these comforts they are becoming slaves to."

Yet as our culture lapses ever more deeply into its obsession with consumption, with things, as it urges upon us new wants and pseudo-needs, promising limitless technological progress and delivering endless distraction, it is surely time to consider where this faith in money and desire for possessions is taking us.

It is also time to consider the value of simplicity, silence and solitude. "Silence," writes Max Picard in *The World of Silence*, "is the only phenomenon today that is 'useless'. It does not fit into the world of profit and utility. It simply is. It seems to have no other purpose; it cannot be exploited. . . . You cannot get anything out of it. It is 'unproductive'. Therefore it is regarded as valueless.

"Yet there is more help and healing in silence than in all the 'useful things'. Purposeless, unexploitable silence, suddenly appears at the side of the all-too-purposeful, and frightens us by its very purposelessness. It interferes with the regular flow of the purposeful. It strengthens the untouchable, it lessens the damage inflicted by exploitation. It makes things whole again, by taking them back from the world of dissipation into the world of wholeness. It gives things something of its own holy uselessness, for that is what silence itself is: holy uselessness."

WORK AS A BANE

Another defining feature of the Modernist attitude to life is its idea of work, and in particular menial and physical work, as an undesirable activity from which we should escape if at all possible. Our culture teaches that the workplace, whether the kitchen sink, the office, the laboratory, the farm or factory, is a place of drudgery and boredom, where labour, rather than being a creative and rewarding experience, is something akin to an oppression. This is certainly true of the millions who consider food preparation and home-making to be undesirable and unfulfilling chores.

There are still, of course, a minority who continue to see their work in terms of a fulfilling vocation—potters and physicians, teachers and midwives, poets and musicians—whose work and leisure, labour and pleasure are woven into a coherent whole. But these are rare; almost an endangered species.

Out of this contempt for work has arisen the idea of labour as primarily a means of acquiring money. I know of several young people who are in highly paid but boring, short contract jobs (invariably to do with computers) which provide them with an income but little satisfaction outside the realms of personal relationships, sport, drink and foreign travel. Their life begins at the end of the working day and at weekends. Trapped in an economic cycle from which they have no ways of escaping, they are the foot soldiers of an army of those who work for only one reason: to fulfil pressing economic commitments—in particular, for the majority, their mortgage.

But this is an army where stress is on the increase; in 2003 it replaced backache as the leading cause for absenteeism in this country, and death from overwork is an increasingly common phenomenon. In Japan they call it *karochi*, and in China it is *guolaosi*. Yet as more and more people put in longer hours and suffer more stress, there may soon arise a word for it in English. The last seven years have seen a significant rise in the number of employees working in excess of 48 hours a week, rising from 10% in the late 1990s to 26% now.[3] The same period has seen a significant rise in clinical obesity and addiction to alcohol.

All the ancient wisdom that has come down to us warns of the folly of this situation. "It tells us," writes Wendell Berry, "that work is necessary to us, as much a part of our condition as mortality; that good work is our salvation and our joy; that shoddy or dishonest or self-serving work is our curse and our doom."

THE CULT OF SPEED

I counted my footsteps to a bush or to some other mark, and this number seemed but a trifle deducted from the sum that lay ahead of us. Yet I had no desire to travel faster. In this way there was time to notice things—a grasshopper under a bush, a dead swallow on the ground, the tracks of a hare, a bird's nest, the shape and colour of ripples on the sand, the bloom of tiny seedlings pushing through the soil. There was time to collect a plant or look at a rock. The very slowness of our march diminished the monotony. I thought how terribly boring it would be to rush about this country in a car.
Wilfred Thesiger

Fast and Slow do more than just describe a rate of change. They are short-hand for ways of being, or philosophies of life. Fast is busy, controlling, aggressive, hurried, analytical, stressed, superficial, impatient, active, quantity-over-quality. Slow is the opposite: calm, careful, receptive, still, intuitive, unhurried, patient, reflective, quality-over-quantity. It is about making real and meaningful connections—with people, culture, work, food, everything.
Carl Honoré

A major feature of Modernism is its attitude to and obsession with speed. It may have begun in the fourteenth century when clocks were first erected in public places, but scheduling only became a way of life during the nineteenth, when industrial capitalism fed on speed and rewarded it with profit. Even today the business that manufactures and sells its products the fastest invariably undercuts its rivals.

"Waste of time," writes Max Weber in *The Protestant Ethic and the Spirit of Capitalism*, "is the first and in principle the deadliest of sins. . . . Loss of time through sociability, idle talk, luxury, even more sleep than is necessary for health . . . is worthy of absolute moral condemnation."

Yet although the spirit of nineteenth-century capitalism encouraged the cult of speed, impatience and haste have subsequently invaded every corner of life, domestic no less than industrial. Every new technological invention—the railway, the plane, the motor car, the mobile telephone, the internet, even the microwave—has increased the pressure to live at a faster rate. We now work fast, travel fast, eat fast, cook fast, make decisions in a rush and do more than one thing at a time. Money, too, is speeding up. Consider this: from the beginning of human history to the year 1900, the world economy grew to $600 billion in anual output. Today, the world economy grows by this amount every two years. More than $2 trillion circulates around the world every day. Thus money is commanding ever more of our attention, and compromising our ability to control our destinies. Stress, hypertension, insomnia, migraines, asthma and gastrointestinal troubles are some of the consequences.

But I don't think our mania for speed is solely attributable to capitalism. Part of the problem is our alienation from nature. Part, too, our desire to anaesthetise the soullessness of the modern world. "Our period," Milan Kundera writes, "is obsessed with the desire to forget, and it is to fulfil that desire that it gives over to the demon of speed; it picks up the pace to show us that it no longer wishes to be remembered, that it is tired of itself; that it wants to blow out the tiny trembling flame of memory."

Yet there are signs of a belated reaction. The Slow Food Movement, founded by Carlo Petrini in 1986, is a call to arms against the cult of speed in all its forms. As its name suggests, it stands for everything that the fast food restaurants do not: fresh, local, seasonal produce; recipes handed down from generation to generation; sustainable farming; leisurely preparation of food; and slow dining. There is also a *Citta Slow* or Slow Cities movement, which has more than thirty member towns in Italy and beyond.

But deceleration, like charity, best begins at home. The virtues of slowness—better health, better work, better business, better family life, better sex and friendships—can be discovered on a daily basis simply by attending to our own behaviour. The first step is to relax—put aside impatience, stop rushing and learn to accept imperfection and inaction. Then remove the wristwatch and become more mindful of the world around you; slow down and learn to gaze, slow down and listen, take longer over everything, eat without rushing, linger, drive within the speed limit, learn to do things for their own sake. But the battle against speeding does not imply that everything should be done at a snail's pace; some activities require speed. The arts of life include *presto* as well as *lento* and *larghetto*.

For all this, our best tutors are undoubtedly the animals—the domestic cat, for example. Observe how it runs at ninety miles an hour and then nonchalantly saunters past; how it springs and then lazes in the sun; never rushed, never driven, never pushing against the clock. "With my cats," writes Jeffrey Masson, "I am learning the lesson of the sufficiency of the moment. No yesterday, no tomorrow, only the magic of today, of this single instant. No remorse, no regret, no yearning, just the play of now." That's living.

ESCAPING THE FAST LIFE, THE NOISY LIFE, THE RELENTLESS PACE OF MODERNISM

> I am not One who much or oft delight
> To season my fireside with personal talk,—
> Of friends, who live within an easy walk,
> Or neighbours, daily, weekly, in my sight:
> And, for my chance acquaintance, ladies bright.
> Sons, mothers, maidens withering on the stalk,
> These all wear out of me, like Forms, with chalk
> Painted on rich men's floors, for one feast-night.
> Better than such discourse doth silence long,
> Long, barren silence, square with my desire;
> To sit without emotion, hope, or aim,
> In the loved presence of my cottage-fire,
> And listen to the flapping of the flame,
> Or kettle whispering its faint undersong.
> *William Wordsworth*

Does it matter? Does the loss of silence and solitude really matter? Are we better, happier people in a quiet place, or morally improved by solitude? Have we been lessened by the fact that solitude, silence and slowness are now so often out of our reach? It is the simple premise of this book that this is so.

There are, I suggest, several reasons for this conclusion, which fly in the face of contemporary assumptions. The majority of young people seeking the fast life are attracted to cities where they may enjoy it. They don't favour introspection, and seek sensual gratification whenever possible; self-discipline, discretion, modesty and reticence are anathema. Loud music is preferred to quiet, violence to calmness, speed to shanks's pony, Peckinpah's *Straw Dogs* to Ray's *Pather Panchali*.

Yet such restlessness is a relatively new phenomenon, characteristic of Modernism, of adolescent energies and the speed of machinery, rather than, say, the slower pace of the pre-industrial eras, when the fastest thing was a running horse and the loudest a thunderclap. Yes, although that period could be violent and venal, greedy and hypocritical, it was also quiet. The countryside was relatively peaceful, and so was the culture: no throbbing music, no hectic traffic, no fast-paced commercials or endlessly restless movement. People lived reflectively and, in general, at peace with themselves.

We are, I believe, lessened by restlessness because our culture's emphasis on quick gratification is always forcing us to look ahead to the next pleasure—ideal perhaps for those who are in the business of running a commercial enterprise, but less satisfactory for those who are not. In these circumstances, the consumer's enjoyment, being hurried, even snatched, is more superficial, less imaginative, than one enjoyed slowly and in depth. One of the principal benefits of a slow, contemplative pleasure is that it nurtures the soul; the satisfaction of speed is less lasting, less profound and more superficial. A reflective person is able to look backwards and is less likely to make mistakes; an unreflective person is always looking forwards towards the next and better fix.

In my view, the fully active life, if necessary and often hugely stimulating, always needs, like the fallow year that follows a period of intensive agriculture, a period of rest.

We all need time not only for reflection, but for relaxation. We need time to renew ourselves, to strengthen our depleted resources. And if this has been true in the past, it has never been more so than in our own time—demanding and greedy as it is. We need silence as an antidote to the clamour, solitude as a barrier against the distractions, and slowness as a cure for the current speed of life.

CHAPTER FOUR

Tools for Re-enchantment

The distortions and delusions, the stresses and exhaustions I have been describing need to be counteracted if we are to be free from restlessness, agitation and overwork. The pursuit of contentment, creativity and refreshment of spirit should be our objective.

Refreshment is of key importance in lives so often burdened with pressures and responsibilities, whose demands shut down imagination and creative energy. Many of us enjoy leisure, comfort and affluence, but have yet to find a way of discovering a life characterised by deep-seated well-being. Instead our lives are marked by a void at their centres.

Perhaps, then, some of the following suggestions addressed to those in search of greater fulfilment might be of value.

THE ART OF THE COMMONPLACE

I have learned from long experience that there is nothing that is not marvellous and that the saying of Aristotle is true—that in every natural phenomenon there is something wonderful, nay, in truth, many wonders. We are born and placed among wonders and surrounded by them, so that to whatever object the eye first turns, the same is wonderful and full of wonders, if only we will examine it for a while.

John de Dondis

Fine dancing, I believe, like virtue, must be its own reward.

Jane Austen

The ordinary moments of our daily life may appear commonplace, but in reality they are not so; they carry enormous significance. To polish a pair of shoes, to serve a helping of apple pie, to break bread, to chop firewood—these can be lordly activities. Any action performed with a sense of reverence, of care and of pleasure, can become what I would call a sacrament.

Zen, in particular, lays emphasis on 'everyday life' as the real path to the great mystery. One of its Masters, Joshu, replied to a question about the true nature of the Great Way, the Tao, by saying, "Our everyday life, that is the Tao." It is the worship of the moment's duration, inviolate, detached, and passionate. It is the observation of the sunlight on a blade of grass, the sight of a beetle crawling across a leaf; the worship of the day's most commonplace events:

> I draw water,
> I carry wood,
> This is my magic.

In a religious culture, one in which God's name has real significance and is regularly invoked, every action, however humble, is offered for His sake and His alone. The poet George Herbert gives expression to this invocation in his beautiful poem, 'The Elixir':

> Teach me, my God and King,
> In all things thee to see,
> And what I do in any thing,
> To do it as for thee . . .

> A man that looks on glasse,
> On it may stay his eye;
> Or if he pleaseth, through it passe,
> And then the heav'n espie . . .

> A servant with this clause
> Makes drudgerie divine:
> Who sweeps a room, as for thy laws,
> Makes that and th'action fine.

> This is the famous stone
> That turneth all to gold:
> For that which God doth touch and own
> Cannot for lesse be told.

The Indian sage and social reformer Vinoba Bhave (1895–1982), no less imbued by a sense of the divine, also recorded his conviction that an action dedicated to the Lord—in his case the Lord Krishna—was its own reward. "If a farmer serves his cattle with this noble *bhavana* (deep feeling of reverence), even this ordinary work of his becomes worship of the Lord.

In the same way, if the mistress of the household tries to feed and please the family by keeping the kitchen clean, lighting the fire and preparing pure and wholesome food, all these acts of hers are *yajna*, sacrificial action."

But of course in the UK we no longer live in a culture where work is undertaken in a spirit of service that moves towards the kind of timelessness implicit in his words; farmers in the West do not 'serve' their animals, nor do homemakers maintain their houses as a sacrificial action. The majority see work as an unpalatable but necessary chore. With this dispiriting notion most people live their lives. Nonetheless, it is not impossible to perform every kind of act, however commonplace, in a manner conducive to the reverential spirit described by George Herbert and Vinoba Bhave. But to do so we need to make a simple but revolutionary shift of viewpoint: to replace all those lingering angers, all those choking resentments, all that restlessness, with a calm acceptance of our prospects for the future, a sense of gratitude for life's varied and manifold gifts, and a determination to fulfil our work to the best of our ability.

There are certain calming activities whose pursuit is more conducive to *bhavana* than others. These include the nation's most popular and widespread leisure activity, gardening. Other equally calming pursuits include needlework and flower arranging, making and listening to music, and baking. Another especially rewarding activity is the conscious creation of a lovely environment: a home can be a continuous refreshment, a harvest of delight and creativity.

One who experienced his home in terms of such delight was the painter Pierre Bonnard (1867–1947), whose subject matter was that which lay immediately to hand. In 1926 he purchased a modest late 19th-century dwelling, the Villa du Bosquet above Le Cannet on the French Côte d'Azur; the house and its immediate environment supplied the painter with the subject matter he required.

By choice Bonnard lived simply with few luxuries, apart from a modern bathroom and a car. Visitors to Le Bosquet were invariably struck by the simplicity of the furnishings and by the small 'impractical and uncomfortable workroom' that was his studio. His nephew Charles Terrace once likened the painter's bedroom to a monastic cell.

The silence of these rooms evokes the anonymous self-portrait he once gave a French journal: "The artist who paints the emotions creates an enclosed world—the picture—which, like a book, has the same interest no matter where it happens to be. Such an artist, we may imagine, spends a great deal of time doing nothing but look, both around and inside him."

Bonnard never ceased to look—and celebrate what he saw. He took daily walks with his pet dachshund, Pouchette, in the villa's garden and the surrounding country with its pine, almond and mimosa trees and vineyards. "Art will never be able to exist without nature," he said. But it was the house that claimed his most affectionate attention. He made paintings of almost every one of its rooms, joyously celebrating their small, rather bare spaces: 59 pictures of the dining room; 21 of the small sitting room; 15 of the tiny bathroom; 11 of the studio; and of the garden, yet 19 more. The Villa's commonplace contents—its cupboards, bathtub, face flannel, radiators, table and chairs—were painted with no less affection. Yet Bonnard's visions, unlike those of Odilon Redon or William Blake, did not come to him as apparitions—he saw them all around him. His sitting room, his garden, some bowls of fruit, some vases of flowers, blaze with transfiguring insight, for Bonnard experienced the ecstatic vision of the ordinary which mescaline eaters are said to achieve.

According to the Gnostic Gospel of Thomas, Jesus was asked when the Kingdom would come. "It will not come by waiting for it. . . . Rather, the kingdom of the Father is spread out upon the earth, and men do not see it." Bonnard did.

So did Gerard Manley Hopkins, who regretted that although "there lives the dearest freshness deep down things," few experienced it for themselves. "I thought how sadly beauty of inscape was unknown and buried away from simple people and yet how near at hand it was if they had eyes to see it and it could be called out everywhere again," he wrote.

But if you are of a mind to discover this "beauty of inscape" for yourself, consider reading some of Hopkins's exultant verses: for example 'The May Magnificat', 'Pied Beauty' and 'Hurrahing in Harvest'. Here is the first stanza of his poem celebrating the miracle of spring.

> Nothing is so beautiful as spring—
>> When weeds, in wheels, shoot long and lovely and lush;
>> Thrush's eggs look like little low heavens, and thrush
> Through the echoing timber does so rinse and wring

The ear, it strikes like lightnings to hear him sing;
  The glassy peartree leaves and blooms, they brush
  The descending blue; that blue is all in a rush
With richness; the racing lambs too have fair their fling

Alternatively, you might have a mind to look at other celebrations of the festival of life that are to be found in paintings. I love Rembrandt's etching of 1650, with the mottled shell resting in a pool of its own shadow; I love Chardin's *Basket of Wild Strawberries*, with its lustrous blood-red pyramid of fruit and, no less powerful and beautiful, I love van Gogh's famous painting of a pair of old shoes. I also love the land-scapes of Caspar David Friedrich and the interiors by Gwen John, no less imbued with an atmosphere of silence. "Solitude is essential to my conversation with nature," said Friedrich, and John, a recluse, would have said no less.

The beginning of *seeing* lies with the rapt observation of unpreten-tious, everyday things; things ignored, mundane, unexceptional, com-monplace; things lying about in rooms, things like the wrinkled sheets on an unmade bed, the refracted stems of a bunch of tulips in a glass pot, the rust on a sheet of corrugated iron, the pattern of porridge left at the bottom of an unwashed pan. Looking requires no dogmas, demands no set faith. It stipulates only one thing—a sensual commit-ment to each passing moment, without reserve or calculation.

Van Gogh's contemporary, the painter Claude Monet (1840–1926), was as much in love with the natural world as his friend Bonnard. Perhaps he was an even greater celebrant—the greatest *seer* of all time.

Monet delighted in the glory of being alive—the incredible chance of it! He took delight in the quivering and shivering leaves of a row of poplars along the banks of the River Epte, the reflection of clouds in the water of his garden at Giverny, the façade of Rouen cathedral lit by the red light of the setting sun, and the cool, white, early morning mists rising from the still waters of the River Seine. He saw dawns and dusks, sunrises and twilights, spring and winter, ice flows and flowering mead-ows with an unprejudiced eye that can startle by the truth of its veracity to the spectacle of precarious life. In nature he saw the glory of the earth. There his culture had the greatest flowering and continuity, and there he was inspired to offer praise for the miracle of sight.

As far as I know, Monet held no religious beliefs—he may have been an atheist—yet the corpus of his work is one long song of exultation for the mystery upon mystery of creation, a *Benedicite*, such as that sung in both East and West in the Office of Laud, a comprehensive liturgy of the universe: "O ye Winter and Summer, bless ye the Lord: praise him and magnify him for ever. O ye Dews and Frosts, bless ye the Lord: praise him and magnify him for ever."

Monet wished, he told Lilla Cabot Perry, "that he had been born blind and then had suddenly gained his sight so that he could have begun to paint . . . without knowing what the objects were that he saw before him."

To see the visible world in all its grandeur with his lyrical intensity we too have to escape from the petty preoccupations of our immediate surroundings and enjoy our own poetic vision. The power of imagination is to see things in their eternal aspect; it is to know the timeless as it 'moves through time', the eternal presence that is both in and outside time.

CREATIVITY

Mental health is characterised by the ability to love and to create.
Erich Fromm

The passion for form is a way of trying to find and constitute meaning in life. And this is what genuine creativity is. Imagination, broadly defined, seems to me to be a principle of human life underlying even reason, for the rational functions . . . can participate in the constituting of reality—only as they are creative. Creativity is thus involved in our every experience as we try to make meaning of our self–world relationship.
Rollo May

To create presupposes delight—an exhilaration—in *making* as the expression of our deepest nature, the part of us with the most intrinsic value. To live the self-expressive life, the creative life, is to tread a path towards the deepest personal fulfilment. It is to realise dreams, to be alert to the imagination. It is to partake of the healing power unknown by those who do not have the courage to create. As Rollo May observes, "In human beings courage is necessary to make *being* and *becoming* possible. An assertion of the self, a commitment, is essential if the self is to have any reality."

However, the opposite can be calamitous: to work at something in which one has little or no belief, no commitment, no delight—'it's just a job. I do it for the money'—is to bring about an incorrigible paralysis of one's personal well-being, an inner death, a throttling of life's most vivid aspirations. In the powerful words of Charles Dickens, it is to make "a coffin of the heart".

To live creatively is to touch *everything* with joyful, unexpected magic. It is to nourish the children's bedtime stories with fresh invention; to delight visitors with an astonishing dish served on a carefully laid table; to enrich the garden with unheard of combinations of plants; to enchant a room with decoration and colour; to paint pictures, make music, write poems, to play with life. The playful life is one intoxicated by spirit, at once unselfconscious and spontaneous, yet disciplined.

We should reject the mass taste of those who imitate rather than invent. Living is an art, in fact the most important and at the same time the most difficult and complex art to be practised by anybody. To give expression to something personal, however modest, is one of its supreme satisfactions.

GRATITUDE AND PRAISE

Without a sense of wonder one has lost not only the spoor of life but the power of true increase.
Laurens van der Post

The great work of the solitary life is gratitude.
Thomas Merton

The further I advance into solitude the more clearly I see the goodness of things.
Thomas Merton

The great Christian societies were always characterised by a culture of gratitude and praise. Such at least is the evidence from the Hebridean islands of Scotland which stretch out into the Atlantic, immense expanses of barren, treeless and rocky terrain. Their inhabitants, crofters and fishers by day, spent their evenings "telling tales and histories, invocations and prayers, singing hymns and songs, runes and lays, sweet, beautiful and soft." These are the words of the Celtic scholar Alexander Carmichael (1832–1912), who spent a lifetime collecting their prayers, songs and poetry. The fruit of his work, the six-volume *Carmina Gadelica*, is an unrivalled treasury of the generosity of Celtic spirituality.

As Carmichael found, the inhabitants of these remote isles lived in a natural state of innocent prayer—prayers from birth to death, from dawn to dusk, from the start of the year until its close—prayer informed by gratitude to their Creator. It was a praying, says Esther de Waal, which responded to, and grew out of, their way of life:

> What they said and sung—for these prayers were also hymns and poetry, the two cannot be separated—grew out of their sense of the presence of God as the most immediate reality in their lives. Religion permeated everything they did. They made no distinction between the secular and the sacred. . . . They felt totally at home with God.

On going into their houses, Carmichael was struck to hear how they addressed the "great God of life, Father of all living". Catherine Maclennan told him:

> My mother would be asking us to sing our morning song to God down in the back-house, as Mary's lark was singing it up in the clouds and as Christ's mavis was singing it yonder in the tree, giving glory to the God of the creatures for the repose of the night, for the light of the day, and for the joy of life. She would tell us that every creature on the earth here below and in the ocean beneath and in the air above was giving glory to the great God of the creatures and the worlds, of the virtues and the blessings, and would we be dumb.

Such gratitude comes from the heart; it is a song of delight in the wonders of existence; an outpouring of appreciation for the gifts of food, shelter, sunlight, other people, life itself. But since the Education Act of 1880, the development of industrialism and the lessening of Christian faith, that sense of gratitude, once so widespread, has largely atrophied. We hear it when an audience registers its appreciation for a great performance, and in the voice of a patient thanking the nurse for her caring, but it is no longer a commonly felt thing. We are more knowing, greedier and less grateful, taking wealth and privilege for granted.

Yet when the heart melts in love it becomes a habit of mind to praise the workings of nature: the rain, the worms in the soil, the trees which give us shade and beauty, the squirrels which damage them but give us back their acrobatics; the good works of our friends and those we do not know.

It can become a simple habit of mind to express our gratitude for every aspect of life—something which found its loving expression in the exultant praise, offering adoration, of St Francis's great Canticle of 1220:

> Thank you, my God, for the moon and the stars;
> You have formed them in the sky, clear, precious and beautiful.
> Thank you, my Lord, for Brother Wind
> And for the air, cloudy and serene, and all weather,
> By which you give your children sustenance.
> Thank you, my God, for Sister Water,
> Who is very useful and soothing and precious and pure.

I am writing this book in my mid-seventieth year, and am conscious that my stay on Earth must sooner or later come to its end. How many more times will I see the swallows returning, will I hear thunder over the hills, will I walk along the margin of the incoming sea, or taste the flavour of cheddar cheese? How many more times will I encounter my four sons, three grandsons and wife of almost fifty years? When I was much younger I took living all for granted. I was too busy with my own affairs. Now I feel differently. I have discovered an obligation to each fleeting moment. I recognise that life is a miracle and my appreciation grows with my diminishing opportunities to experience it. This is the gift of age.

THE HEALING POWER OF NATURE

If you wish to advance into the infinite, explore the finite in all directions.
Johann Wolfgang von Goethe

We need the tonic of wildness,—to wade sometimes in marches where the
bittern and the meadow-hen lurk, and hear the booming of the snipe; to
smell the whispering sedge where only some wilder and more solitary fowl
builds her nest, and the mink crawls with its belly close to the ground. At the
same time that we are earnest to explore and learn all things, we require that
all things be mysterious and unexplorable, the land and sea be infinitely wild,
unsurveyed and unfathomed by us because unfathomable. We can never have
enough of Nature. We must be refreshed by the sight of the inexhaustible
vigour, vast and Titanic features, the sea-coast with its wrecks, the wilderness
with its living and decaying trees, the thunder cloud, and the rain which lasts
three weeks and produces freshets. We need to see our own limits trans-
gressed, and some life pasturing freely where we never wander.
Henry David Thoreau

Another powerful antidote to consumerism's lure is to be found in
nature—to which, it has been said, one can attach fifty-two different
meanings! Here I mean by nature those parts of the visible world which
were not humanly created, and are perceived through the senses: the
breeze on our face, the weed in the edge of the pavement, the Ruisdael-
like clouds behind a grove of wintry trees, the vermilion-red geranium
on the window sill, the ice flowers on a window, no less than mountains, oceans and the open spaces of the countryside—anything that is
organic and unselfconscious.

Yet assuredly, although we may be living in a built environment
without trees and fields, we may yet be closer to nature than we at first
suppose. There is the glow of the afternoon's sun on the neighbour's
chimney pot, the sound of birds twittering in sheltered squares, and the
presence of inquisitive, bright-eyed children playing their complicated
games with complete absorption. Then perhaps the sunrise. Draw back
the bedroom curtains and wonder at the morning's gift of the newly
born sun bubbling over the horizon—this morning a gleaming phos-
phorescent carmine, yesterday a hot bulb of iridescent light, and the

day before, a cloudscape of thickly curdled brass. How great is this gift, the first of the day's sensations! The sunrise and clouds can be seen over town and country alike.

To escape the bias of modernity, make a point of seeking refreshment in nature, wherever you live. I can gaze across the Atlantic ocean from the Cornish cliffs, or walk through the woods beside the river Torridge. If they are carpeted with wild flowers, if they are chiming with the songs of birds, if they are ancient, mossy and verdant, so much the better, but the sight of the river gleaming in soft sunlight will be sufficient; one glimpse of it will be enough. But if I now lived (as I once lived) in the red brick streets of a northern town—it was Wakefield—there are still sights to be enjoyed, scents to be relished, sounds to be heard and cherished. The song of a thrush will be enough. And as Monet knew, one tree, one cloud or reflection will be enough to slake one's thirst for the beauty of the wild.

Here, the diarist James Lees-Milne glories in the beauty of a single dandelion flower:

> I lay on the grass and peered closely in the head of one. It was like looking into the inmost recesses of the sun, a swirl with petal flames alive and licking each other. To think that each of the billion dandelions in Buckinghamshire, which are taken for granted or ignored, is in fact a marvellous star of golden beauty. How blind human beings are to the best around them, and perceptive of the worst.
>
> *James Lees-Milne*

THE IMPORTANCE OF RELATIONSHIP

Omnia vincit Amor: et nos cedamus Amori
(Love conquers all things: let us too give in to love)
Virgil

Countless surveys reach a similar conclusion: that the key consideration in the avoidance of wretchedness, of a sense of futility, even depravity, involves the quality and meaning of human relationships. Those people who care about others, the surveys inform us, are on average happier than those who are more preoccupied with themselves. The truth of this observation cannot be doubted.

Love is the key to the doors of tenderness, relationship and unity. And by love I don't solely mean that of the Romeo and Juliet variety— a more or less short-lived romantic or sexual attachment—but also, and more particularly, a life-long attachment to somebody else. To be loved and to love in return is possibly the greatest source of happiness that most of us can ever know. The experience of sharing, of intimacy, of communion, encourages the uninhibited unfolding of one's inner life.

Nonetheless, our culture's insistence on supportive and rewarding human attachments, especially sexual fulfilment, continues to obscure the importance of love and reverence for non-human creatures, such as animals. It may also obscure the fact that there is nothing perverse about getting away from others. Some people—and there are lots of them—find enjoyment in living on their own.

But in extending our love to animals we need, I suggest, not only to consider our dogs, budgerigars or hamsters, but those whom we currently regard as our slaves and regularly slaughter to eat—cows, sheep, chickens and fish.

LIVING IN THE MOMENT

If by eternity is understood not endless temporal duration but timelessness, then he lives eternally who lives in the present.
Ludwig Wittgenstein

Give me nothing fixed, set, static. Don't give me the infinite or the eternal: nothing of infinity, nothing of eternity. Give me the still, white seething, the incandescence and coldness of the incarnate moment: . . . the immediate present, the Now.
D. H. Lawrence

How is it that those who are alive can never realise their chance beyond all chances, how is it that even the wisest of us are such fools that we take our

hour of exemption from nothingness for granted; giving to the moments that
race past at best but a listless attention!
Llewelyn Powys

Being successful in life does not necessarily consist of acquiring possessions, but of the employment of the free, healthy life of the senses and
the imagination. "It is," says the novelist John Cowper Powys, "to use
your will to force the passing moment to become a medium for the
eternal. It is to get hold of the moment by its throat. . . . Rape the
moment as it passes," he advises. "It can never pass again; and for all
you know its very drabness may prove a loophole into the eternal if you
press against it hard enough."

Like others, I spend the greater part of my days in a kind of never-
never land of semi-conscious awareness. Yes, I can see it's a fine day,
that the sun is shining and, when I look, I can see bright clouds in the
sky. The cat's black fur is glistening and the flowering cherry is splendid. But—but—in truth I have not been paying attention to the reality
of this room and the view beyond its window. I'm not really *experiencing* what is right here in front of me and doing so without interpreta-
tion, comment and judgement. I'm not really in contact with what has
been happening in these present moments. I'm not really accepting this
room, this space, this light, this cat, and allowing them just to be, to be
themselves. Just *being*. I've let these precious, unrepeatable moments
pass by without attention. "One lives so badly," observed the poet
Rainer Maria Rilke, "because one always comes into the present unfinished, unable, distracted."

It seems easier, more comfortable, to live in a state of somnambu-
lism, to take the fleeting experience for granted, to lose oneself in the
past or in the future, than to follow the path of what Buddhists describe
as 'mindfulness'. Yet the alternative to such thoughtless living is not a
difficult one: it is to take conscious delight in moments of contemplative ecstasy. It is to pay alert attention to every moment; so that planting these brassicas is as good a moment for wonder as entering Santa
Sophia.

The exiled Vietnamese monk Thich Nhat Hanh reiterates a similar
theme: "Life," he writes, "can be found only in the present moment
because 'the past no longer is' and the future has 'not yet come.'

Buddhahood, liberation, awakening, peace, joy, and happiness can be found in the present moment. The place of our appointment is right here, in this very place."

In *Our Appointment with Life*, Thich Nhat Hanh makes the suggestion that we might undertake certain everyday activities such as drinking a cup of tea in a 'mindful' state of mind. "When our mind and our body are fully in the present moment, then the tea appears clearly to us. We know it is a wonderful aspect of existence. At that time we are really in contact with the cup of tea. It is only at times like this that life is really present." Of course, this mindful attentiveness does not need to be restricted to the drinking of a cup of tea; anything rooted in the immediacy of experience can be undertaken in such a way that we become aware and alert to the moment of life itself. "Observe deeply what is happening in the present moment," said the Buddha, "but do not become attached to it."

The American writer John Daniel expresses this well:

The point is here and now. I look out on these trees, this landscape ridged and furrowed by time, and I see not intent but accomplishment, not disarray but order, not insensate matter but spirited meaning. I see such fullness of meaning that my heart aches with it. This is the gift, the given world. To accept it, to bear the privilege of being, is to belong to a majesty we can't comprehend. In the end, we can only be grateful.

To be conscious of the wonders of the 'really' present, we need to become aware of where we are; the space around us, the light which fills it, the colours and textures of the surrounding environment, the shape of the bright gold sun patch on the wall, the way the light illuminates each chrome bar of the gas heater or the curvature of the arms of this upholstered chair. Being in contact with life in this awakened state, you can be alone and fully alive even in a crowd. This is a centred stillness from which 'oneself' can be extracted from all attachments and distractions. This is where I am, and glad I am to be here.

To achieve such concentration is not an easy task; the mind has its compulsions to wander. It has its own circuitous, unpredictable, unruly paths—to become impatient, irritable, confused. But to avoid this snare, retrace your steps calmly, attentively and without haste. Come back to the present; accept the meander as a diversion and pick up the path at the point where it was left behind. Then experience the present emptied of thoughts; experience it without confusion—in itself. Float on the experience, the sensation itself. Annie Dillard suggests how this can be:

> This is it, I think, this is it, right now, the present, this empty gas station, here, this western wind, this tang of coffee on the tongue, and I am patting the puppy, I am watching the mountain. And the second I verbalise this awareness in my brain, I cease to see the mountain or feel the puppy. I am opaque, so much black asphalt.

The delight in life she describes can be experienced when we give life its space, its focused contemplation—it is an experience that can never be rushed, that cannot be snatched, that is never forgotten.

As Thich Nhat Hanh says, "People usually consider walking on water or in thin air a miracle. But I think the real miracle is not to walk on water or thin air, but to walk on earth. Every day we are engaged in a miracle which we don't even recognise: a blue sky, white clouds, green leaves, the black, curious eyes of a child—our own two eyes. All is miracle."

LOOKING FOR THE BEAUTIFUL

> The soul is nurtured by beauty. What food is to the body, arresting, complex, and pleasing images are to the soul.
> *Thomas Moore*

> Xerxes, I read, "halted his unwieldy army for days that he might contemplate to his satisfaction" the beauty of a single sycamore.
> *Annie Dillard*

> The greatest thing a human soul ever does in this world is to see something, and tell what it saw in a plain way. Hundreds of people can talk for one who can think, but thousands can think for one who can see. To see clearly is poetry, prophesy, and religion—all in one.
> *John Ruskin*

It tells us a lot about our culture that the idea of the 'beautiful' is so often perceived to be an embarrassment; not perhaps when it is used as a description of an attractive girl, but one to be avoided in more utilitarian contexts such as the architecture of a hospital or the headquarters of a bank. Nor would it be appropriate to use it in connection with the typography of a tax form or the design of a shop fascia. A newly built housing estate may be advertised as 'prestigious', 'luxurious', 'exclusive', but never in my experience as 'beautiful'. It's a small but revealing demonstration of the priorities which underlie our values, because the beautiful was not only once highly esteemed, but continues to remain one of life's most glorious refreshments.

Aesthetic discernment was as important among the Japanese of the Heian period (794–1185) as was good grammar in the eighteenth century in this country. Writing as late as 1931, George B. Sansom went so far as to state that the Japanese "habit of finding pleasure in common things, their quick appreciation of form and colour, their feeling for simple elegance, are gifts which may well be envied by us who depend so much for our pleasures upon quantities of possessions and complexity of apparatus." Is the same true of contemporary Japan? I have to say that I doubt it.

Nonetheless, however unrecorded, the 'beautiful' has never ceased to be; its existence is universal and only waiting to be revealed. Van Gogh saw heaven in an uninterrupted patch of grasses (*Meadow with Butterflies*, in the National Gallery), and Stanley Spencer found it in a pile of rusting scrap metal (*The Scrapheap*) as well as in dozens of other insignificant scenes—rubble and dilapidated garden sheds, unrecorded rubbish and so forth. These he painted with a compelling intensity, believing that every material thing, however insignificant, would ultimately be redeemed.

Why ignore this gift of life? Why spend our days with eyes and heart closed to the world? Why not pursue the beautiful with the cunning and determination of a hunter stalking game? To do so, one has only to cease to look with a practical or utilitarian intent and learn to look disinterestedly. Act unhurriedly; slow down to gaze; stop and contemplate. And then relish the sighting.

The beautiful is the daily face of things lurking behind their commonplace exterior. This journey of empathy is also one of re-enchantment.

Another way of familiarising oneself with the beauty of the material world is to look at the work of certain painters—Vermeer, Corot and Winifred Nicholson come to mind, but there are many others—and study how they saw the beautiful in commonplace things.

A different kind of beauty is to be discovered in the realm of music, which offers, as the composer James MacMillan says, "a counter-cultural challenge to the values of our modern age". He continues, "At a time when we find it impossible to make time for any sort of real concentration and reflection, I see music making—whether creating something new, or preserving something past—as a beacon in a de-sensitised and desacralised world. We need to discover a sense of the sacred in the world in order to experience life in its fullness."

I have discovered this in many pieces of music, but for the moment two in particular come to mind, little known but of transcendent purity: Arvo Pärt's exquisitely serene *Spiegel im Spiegel* for piano and violin, and *A Gate into Infinity* by the Japanese Somei Satoh, no less powerful, mysterious and slow-tempoed.

There is nothing I can say about these pieces except that they journeyed with me along the path of silence into regions of the heart I had never previously encountered. They revealed, in the words of composer Einojuhani Rautavaara, "glimpses of eternity through the window of time".

THE MEDITATIVE APPROACH

All worldly pursuits have but one unavoidable and inevitable end, which is sorrow: acquisitions end in dispersion; buildings in destruction; meetings in separation; births in death. Knowing this, one should from the very first renounce acquisition and heaping-up. . . . Life is short, and the time of death is uncertain; so apply yourself to meditation . . .
Milarepa

Another method of lightening the burden of a rampant commercialism lies in the practice of meditation, or if not literally that, the practice of a meditative attitude to life. To find the reality of oneself, as Emily Dickinson and Henry David Thoreau did, it is helpful to live a life unbounded by desire; one that is calm, unhurried, reflective and imaginative. Minimise distractions and restlessness; concentrate on the pursuit and mastery of a particular mental and emotional goal, a goal whose realisation could become the fulfilment of one's life. In other words, seek to live a life of quality rather than one based on quantity.

A meditative approach is an attitude of mind rather than a method, a path rather than a procedure. In consequence, it's more likely that the work of a gardener, a calligrapher or angler, a musician or a masseur, will be conducive to the spirit of the meditative life than, say, a Stock Exchange trader, a racing driver or a US Marine in action in the field. However, it does not necessarily follow that the life of a nun is more soulful than that of an explorer, or the life of a priest more spiritual than that of a poet. When you are truly absorbed in an action, when you are forgetting the self in the act of uniting with something else, when you are forgetting hang-ups, delusions and compulsive attachments, you are already on the way to living the contemplative life. In his book *Zen Mind, Beginner's Mind*, Shunryu Suzuki evokes the attitude which is the usual prelude to the enjoyment of peace of mind. "In activity there should be calmness, and in calmness there should be activity. Calmness and activity are not different."

Meditation is non-credal; it has nothing to do with a religion of any kind. It can be learnt and practised by anyone without distinction of colour, country and belief. Nor has it to do with any particular goal, and certainly not the contemplation of eternal questions. It has nothing to do with thought of any kind—with anything at all, in fact, but intuiting the true nature of existence.

The daily practice of meditation can bring significant emotional, mental and spiritual benefits. It is the perfect antidote to the wages of a world captivated by materialism. And it is, of course, silent.

NEGATIVE CAPABILITY

I discovered that it is necessary, absolutely necessary, to believe in nothing. . . .
No matter what god or doctrine you believe in, if you become attached to it,
your belief will be based more or less on a self-centred idea.
D. T. Suzuki

A Poet is the most unpoetical of any thing in existence; because he has no
Identity—he is continually informing and filling some other Body—The
Sun, the Moon, the Sea and Men and Women who are creatures of impulse
are poetical and have about them an unchangeable attribute—the Poet has
none; no identity . . .

John Keats

The poet John Keats (1795–1821) famously claimed to be able to feel
complete affinity with a billiard ball. He could conceive its "delight
from its own roundness". When it was raining, he had "the sense of
being drowned and rooted like a grain of wheat". According to
Christopher Bamford, "He sought no happiness beyond the present
mystery." Like a chameleon, without an 'ego', his identity was continually "informing and filling some other body." "Nothing startles me
beyond the Moment," he wrote, "The setting sun will always set me to
rights—or if a sparrow come before my window, I take part in its existence as it picks about the gravel."

In a letter to his brother, Keats wrote that the poet was no one
because he took on the point of view of everyone and everything. That
capacity for ambiguity, he declared, is necessary for all greatness. He
called this state of Zen-like unknowing "Negative Capability". As the
poet tells it, he was walking home from a Christmas pantomime with
two friends. One of these, Dilke, Keats characterised as one who never
felt he had a personal identity unless "he had made up his mind about
everything." He describes Dilke as one who "will never come at a truth
as long as he lives, because he is always at it." Listening to him, Keats
writes:

several things dovetailed in my mind, and at once it struck me what quality
went to form a Man of Achievement. . . .—I mean Negative Capability, that
is, when a man is capable of being in uncertainties, Mysteries, doubts, without any irritable reaching after fact & reason.

Elsewhere, Keats argues, "Let us not therefore go hurrying about and
collecting honey, bee-like buzzing here and there; but let us open our
leaves like a flower and be passive and receptive." He came to believe
that the world was a place for "soul making"; this hard life the only way

for us to become a realised identity.

Christopher Bamford concludes his essay: "Hard though it may be to achieve, there is more to Negative Capability than the mere ability to divest one's consciousness of judgements, desires, and purposes so as to live with mystery. For Keats, Negative Capability is apophatic—a *via negativa*—only with regard to what we know. . . . It is not that Keats does not want to know; he wants to know in a different, purer way. He aspires to a more direct access to reality."

REVERENCE

> Reverential thinking is not a luxury, but a condition of our sanity and grace. Those who cannot think reverentially impoverish their own existence. Thinking as calculation is one thing; thinking objectively according to the requirements of science is another thing. Thinking reverentially when we behold the universe in its intimate aspects, infuse it with our love and feel unity with it, is yet another thing. And what joy it is!
> *Henryk Skolimowski*

In truth we live in the midst of wonders and immensities for which reverence is the only appropriate response. We can but revere the existence of the three hundred billion stars of the Milky Way Galaxy; that the slightly larger Andromeda Galaxy comes to our eyes from 2.5 million light-years away; that the beech tree at the corner of our garden is alive each morning with fluttering birds; and that the veined wings of a dragonfly are miracles of delicate life. To be out of touch with these and similar miracles is to live within a shrunken version of reality.

Reverential living assumes reverence for life, reverence for all living creatures, reverence for the cosmos itself. It is a mysticism based on wonder; one of joyful simplicity and praise.

Let Gerard Manley Hopkins give voice to his reverence for the glory of dappled things in his poem 'Pied Beauty', of 1877.

> Glory be to God for dappled things—
> For skies of couple-colour as a brinded cow;
> For rose-moles all in stipple upon trout that swim;

Fresh-firecoal chestnut-falls; finches' wings;
Landscape plotted and pieced—fold, fallow, and plough;
And all trades, their gear and tackle and trim.

All things counter, original, spare, strange;
Whatever is fickle, freckled (who knows how?)
With swift, slow; sweet, sour; adazzle, dim;
He fathers-forth whose beauty is past change:

                                             Praise him.

SEEING

Other animals do not need a purpose in life. A contradiction to itself, the
human animal cannot do without one. Can we not think the aim of life as
being simply to see?
John Gray

The whole of life lies in the verb seeing.
Pierre Teilhard de Chardin

The real journey of discovery consists not in seeking new landscapes, but in
having new eyes.
Marcel Proust

Active looking and seeing implies experiencing life with care, concentration and enjoyment. That means living deliberately: slow gazing, sustained attention, careful analysis and reverence towards everything that lies around us.

I am walking along a path, a familiar path. The same landscape—the same hills, fields, and woods—I see whenever I choose to pass this way. Suddenly, I am startled by the whirr of an unexpected sound—a great flock of fieldfares (or are they starlings?) flying across my course and settling in the bare branches of a tree. There is a cacophonous twittering and the tree seems to have turned into leaf. My heart is full. It was empty and now it is full. It has discovered the intoxication inherent in such simple, everyday things as a flight of birds crossing my path.

Now as I continue walking, I start to see and hear things of which I was previously unconscious—the sounds of the landscape: traffic moving on a distant road, my footsteps splashing through the puddles and a skylark trilling somewhere in the blue. I see, too, the subtle creams, greys and browns of the clouds. I see the slightly yellowish grass before it turns into the most pungent of greens. I see the dandelion flower at my feet—what amazing construction, and how wonderful is the way its shadow curves across an adjacent bramble branch! If I say, "I see" it is because that is what I do, but I'm not simply a viewer of the landscape; I'm in the landscape and as much a part of it as the skylark.

On one occasion Gerard Manley Hopkins evoked the contour of a distant hill in terms of "slow music", and speaking of a bluebell, he said: "I know the beauty of our Lord by it." Just now I hear the music and know the beauty of this dandelion.

In seeking to see and hear, Hopkins was entering the material world in that state of virgin apprehension that the greatest visionary painters experienced more or less on a daily basis. The poetry of life was their reality, their worship. Perhaps this is how Christ knew that the lilies of the field ("which toil not neither do they spin") were so beautiful "that even Solomon in all his glory was not arrayed like one of these", and how, too, Blake saw "Heaven in a wild flower". It is certainly how in 1506 Leonardo da Vinci experienced a Star of Bethlehem plant among swirling grasses, a branch of blackberry and the head of a bear, which he drew with passionate empathy.

Another example of trembling amazement when face to face with the mysterious beauty of the natural world is to be found in the sky paintings of John Constable. Between October 1820 and October 1822, the period of his life known as his 'skying period', Constable painted no less than 54 studies of cloud formations. A further 68 sky studies attributed to the painter exist, although undated.

Of course, Constable's exceptional interest in skies and cloud formations can be partially explained by the fact that he had worked for at least a year at his father's windmill on East Bergholt Common in Suffolk. He had then a professional's interest in the weather: the ability to forecast the wind speed and the direction and the movement of thunderstorms. In this sense Constable's cloud studies are exceptional on account of the accuracy of their depiction. To take an example: on

September 27th 1821, he made three different cloud studies at different times, all of which refer to previous rain:

September 27th 1821—10 morning, fine morning after Rainy night.
Noon, 27th Septr very bright after rain/ wind West
4, 27 Septr 1821 wood bank of Vale (?warm) & bright after rain

We can learn from this painter's rapt observation of the sky; we can learn to look and record for ourselves, if only mentally, what we have seen. Only this morning I lay in bed startled by a pool of purest cobalt and in the same sky a luminous strip of light cerulean; the clouds, shifting, moving forwards, moving backwards, inconstant. A ribbon of light roseate pink colour above the horizon. Amazing rapture.

But painting and drawing are not the only way we can be helped to see and record what we have observed; a written description can be as effective as a visual record. In fact the two approaches have a great deal in common; both are based on close observation; both are dependent on analysis and memory, both require a passionate empathy. What is the colour of this sea as it approaches the horizon? How can I describe the sound of this crowd? What are the sportsmen wearing? Look; look again, remember, and give expression.

D. H. Lawrence was one who could find words for his incomparable observations of place, the atmosphere of the non-human world. Whatever his arrogance on other subjects (love, literature, politics), in his travel writing (for example *Sea and Sardinia*, *Mornings in Mexico*, *Twilight in Italy*) he became the submissive instrument of an almost superhuman attentiveness. Read, for example, the following description of a scene only momentarily observed from the window of a passing train. It comes from an early novel, *The Trespasser*:

Up towards Arundel the cornfields of red wheat were heavy with gold. It was evening when the green of the trees went out, leaving dark shapes upon the sky; but the red wheat was forged in the sunset, hot and magnificent. Siegmund almost gloated as he smelled the ripe corn, and opened his eyes to its powerful radiation. For a moment he forgot everything, amid the forging of red fields of gold in the smithy of the sunset. Like sparks, poppies blew along the railway banks, a crimson train. Siegmund waited, through the meadows, for the next wheat-field. It came like the lifting of yellow-hot metal out of the gloom of darkened grass-lands.

The second passage had a different origin. It is a lengthy and contemplative account of an experience recollected in tranquillity some thirty or forty years after the event. It is by Marcel Proust and comes from the first volume of his novel, *Remembrance of Things Past: Swann's Way*, written and published before the 1914–18 war.

> . . . I remember having first fallen in love with hawthorns. Not only were they in the church, where, holy ground as it was, we had all of us a right of entry, but arranged upon the altar itself, inseparable from the mysteries in whose celebration they participated, thrusting in among the tapers and sacred vessels their serried branches, tied to one another horizontally in a stiff, festal scheme of decoration still further embellished by the festoons of leaves, over which were scattered in profusion, as over a bridal train, little clusters of buds of a dazzling whiteness. Though I dared not look at it save through my fingers, I could sense that this formal scheme was composed of living things, and that it was Nature herself who, by trimming the shape of the foliage and by adding the crowning ornament of those snowy buds, had made a decoration worthy of what was at once a public rejoicing and a solemn mystery. Higher up on the altar, a flower had opened here and there with a careless grace, holding so unconcernedly, like a final, almost vapourous adornment, its bunch of stamens, slender as gossamer and entirely veiling its corolla, that in following, in trying to mimic to myself the action of their efflorescence, I imagined it as a swift and thoughtless movement of the head, with a provocative glance from her contracted pupils, by a young girl in white, insouciant and vivacious.

In our lifetime we experience countless different scenes, but how many of them can we remember? How many are even seen at the time, glimpsed perhaps—but seen? If you open your eyes and look with wonder, even the detritus in the gutter and the mould on an old wall can be beautiful. Let us give these our gratitude, our joy and wonder, above all our love.

Marcel Proust took particular delight in food, its taste, texture and smell; his novel contains numerous descriptions of it, including the most famous taste in all literature, that of the French cake called the *petite madeleine* which his Aunt Leonie used to give him on Sunday mornings, dipping it first in her own tea.

Without the outlay of a single coin, we can discover some touch of wonder, even ecstasy, in the world around us—the purest gnosis of "just this". Hence Christ's statement, "Except ye be converted, and become as little children, ye shall not enter the kingdom of heaven." Or Hakuin Zenji's, "Nirvana is right here, before our eyes,"—and, I'll add, our ears and noses. How important to relish and enjoy the glow, the glory of being alive, the incredible chance of it!

SIMPLICITY

Always bear in mind that very little indeed is necessary for living a happy life.
Marcus Aurelius

The attraction of simplicity is mysterious because it draws us in a completely opposite direction from where most of the world seems to be going: away from conspicuous display, accumulation, egoism and public visibility— toward a life more silent, humble, transparent, than anything known to the extroverted culture of consumption.
Mark A. Birch

A life of simplicity is always relative; friends who have chosen to grow most of their own food and live a frugal existence are affluent in comparison with the austerities of, say, a landless Indian peasant or a mediaeval Celtic saint. They own furniture and books, suffer no shortage of food, and may even go on holidays. So in proposing the importance of simple living I am not referring to a life of penury but one that has turned its back on the wasteful consumer lifestyle, one that seeks to avoid the sense of dissatisfaction and unrealised potential inherent in a life of purely material excess, one that takes the middle way between self-indulgent opulence and a distressing material poverty. "Voluntary simplicity," I wrote in *Timeless Simplicity*, "is a pathway towards the maintenance of a life that is comfortable but not luxurious, frugal but not pinching, decent but not boring: one that seeks to discard the specialist's divisions between work and life, art and everyday activity."

I argued then as I do now that there are two inescapable reasons for choosing to live a life of relative simplicity; first because it is the royal road to unencumbered contentment. The good life need not be dependent on indulgence; indeed that very indulgence can—and does—prohibit serious personal fulfilment. And secondly because in the long run our present Western way of life will prove to be completely unsustainable. Sooner or later a more frugal lifestyle will be not only desirable—it will be an imperative. Drastic downscaling won't be an issue of conscience or choice, it will be an issue of survival.

WALKING

In the Garden of Eden, Adam and Eve walked in the cool of the evening. From archaic times through prehistory, from the Neolithic through antiquity, through the mediaeval period and the Age of Reason and right until the early years of the twentieth century, men and women walked—walked to their fields (as they are still doing in many other parts of the world), walked to their places of worship and for their water and recreation. Walking was as commonplace as breathing and eating.

Throughout the nineteenth century they continued to do so. William Blake's principal boyhood memory was of solitary walking. He walked to Peckham Rye, walked among the haymakers on the outskirts of London. In his late sixties, Blake was still walking to Hampstead from the Strand every Sunday to visit his friends, the Linnells.

He was not alone. The novels of Jane Austen, Charles Dickens, George Eliot and Thomas Hardy are filled with characters who walk long distances. Blake's contemporaries, Wordsworth and Coleridge, thought nothing of walking up to 20 miles each way for visits to each other's houses in the Lake District. The latter's enjoyment of climbing hills and scaling mountain peaks—evident during his Welsh tour, in the Quantocks and the Hertz mountains—is another instance of his passion for this form of meditative recreation. On one occasion he is reported to have completed a ninety-mile round trip in two consecutive days.

But walking was not only a recreational activity. I have been told of farm workers who daily walked to work from Torrington to Hartland, a distance of some twenty miles by road but shorter as the crow flies. How different that experience would have been to those travelling the same journey by car today! Each sight, each temperature, each smell, with its share of wonder—the tea-coloured waters of the river Torridge, the cool shoals of scented garlic, the foaming cow parsley in the hedges, the skylarks burbling in the sky, the first sight of Lundy on the horizon—inviting the traveller to experience a deeply contemplative mood.

Long contact with the earth, with nature, not as a sightseer but as a pedestrian, induces a mood of the profoundest reverie. There is the foot's contact with the ground, the movement of the torso and the swing of the arms; there is the stimulation of things seen, some near, some far, all varied; the wind on the face, the tired feet. The mind becomes contained in its rhythm—I am as I move. Walking, like breathing, connects you to the Earth; it also provides you with a sense of your own reality.

Of course as I speed along on this road, the A39, in my boxed-in automobile, all this is eliminated. No sights, no smells, no changes of temperature; no rhymthic movement of the body either. We travel by car in order to arrive and not to savour the journey. Walking can be a soul-calming experience, but car driving is unrelaxing, especially so as roads become busier.

Nevertheless, walking as a meditative therapy can sometimes be as enjoyable in a town as in the country, especially in the early summer and in the morning: parks and pavements empty, the new sun glinting in the window panes, the air fresh, the streets without traffic, few people in sight, save maybe a road sweeper in the middle distance.

THE VIRTUES OF SILENCE AND SOLITUDE

Silence reveals itself in a thousand inexpressible forms: in the quiet of dawn, in the noiseless aspiration of trees towards the sky, in the stealthy descent of night, in the silent changing of the seasons, in the falling moonlight, trickling down into the night like a rain of silence, but above all in the silence of the inward soul—all these forms of silence are nameless.

Max Picard

In actual fact, society depends for its existence on the inviolable personal solitude of its members. Society, to merit its name, must be made up, not of numbers, or mechanical units, but of persons. To be a person implies responsibility and freedom, and both these imply a certain interior solitude, a sense of personal integrity, a sense of one's own reality and of one's ability to give oneself to society—or to refuse that gift.

When men are merely submerged in a mass of impersonal human beings pushed around by automatic forces, they lose their true humanity, their integrity, their ability to love, their capacity for self-determination. When society is made up of men who know no interior solitude it can no longer be held together by love: and consequently it is held together by violent and abusive authority.

Thomas Merton

A Bishop who had trained as a psychologist, noticed as a chaplain in the Second World War that although he had come across many fine soldiers, few struck him as spiritual men—he had encountered many more in the navy and airforce. When he questioned them about this the sailors, and particularly the airmen, said they were conscious that the long spells they spent alone scanning the uncluttered spaces of sea and sky, free from the scramble which crowded their day on the ground, gave them a unique chance to contemplate their lives calmly in a wider perspective.

Adrian House

What, then, is the value of silence beyond its obvious calming effect— its gift of tranquillity? I would say it can be described as something that brings us into living contact with the mysterious depths of ourselves, the creative spirit, the mysteries of love. I would say that silence is the foundation of love, for love requires clarity, reflection and a focused awareness.

In silence I have a sense of becoming aware of the ground of my being and the ground of life. In silence I sense my own reality. There is a realisation that you are what you are.

I first experienced something of this kind over forty years ago on night walks in the Surrey countryside and subsequently in the Botswanian and Australian bush, but perhaps never more intensely than in the oasis town of Tabas in the middle of the Iranian desert.

Here was an utter silence, a dizzying solitude, an ear-ringing stillness welling into the black, star-studded night. Here I sensed the heartbeat of the world. It was an experience that so permeated my being that I feel it lies within me, ever present, whenever, as Wordsworth knew, one opens one's heart and mind to it.

But, of course, the quest for solitude and tranquillity is not limited to an experience in the Iranian desert; for millions of meditators it can be discovered in their own rooms. Silent contemplation can be practised almost anywhere; it remains an important feature of contemporary Quaker practice, and is also a central part of the Buddhist tradition. Here, again, the teaching emphasises the need for attentive stillness of mind so that, free of distraction, we come to see things as they really are. The most common form of Buddhist meditation is Mindfulness of Breathing, in which the inflows and outflows of breath are the focus of attention, stilling the mind of its restless chatter, its rush of thoughts and emotions, its uninterrupted mental activity, so that that which is can be fully experienced, unhindered by ignorance, craving or prejudice.

But does it matter if we live continuously surrounded by noise? Does the loss of silence really matter? Are we better, happier people in a quiet place, or morally improved by solitude? Are we lessened by the fact that solitude, silence and slowness are so frequently out of our normal reach? There must be several answers to these questions, but the one I'd choose is probably the simplest: silence can teach us who we are. It can nurture our souls and renew our vision. Humans are diminished, their humanity degraded, when they lose contact with their own interior freedom or when it is taken away from them, voluntarily relinquished or stolen by agitation.

So, in my view, our lives are enhanced by a space for tranquillity; like the seventh day in the Book of Genesis, our souls are re-energised by periods of rest.

But solitude and silence have virtues other than their role as a respite from a too-active life; they can be the gates through which we receive the nourishment of 'otherness'. They can provide us with a direct experience of the palpable materiality of our surroundings.

Thus however gregarious we may be, most of us yearn at times for silence; there will always be moments when we want to be alone, to reflect, to pray, to gaze and work uninterruptedly. This was the case in the past: the Christian hermits of the desert, the Trappists with their rule of silence, the wandering solitaries like Basho with his bamboo hat, his cane stick and cotton bag, all give confirmation of our occasional need to escape the hurly-burly of the everyday world: the stressful office, the crowded streets, the queue at the supermarket and the petrol pump.

And certainly this compulsion for a pause, for space, within our otherwise crowded schedule, is to be found not only amongst monks and scholars, but amongst those engaged in serious creative work. There is the blind Milton in his cottage in Chalfont St Giles where he finished *Paradise Lost*, there is Jane Austen in the cottage in Chawton where she wrote *Emma*, there is Emily Brontë in the parsonage at Haworth where she wrote *Wuthering Heights*, there is Yeats in his tower, Thor Ballylee in Galway, and Dylan Thomas in the Boat House at Laugharne. There is also Thomas Carlyle, who erected a sound-proof room in his house in Cheyne Walk. More recently and especially there is Marcel Proust, who wrote his 1,250,000-word novel, *Remembrance of Things Past*, in the absolute seclusion of a cork-lined room. All demanded, and found, quiet.

Many of the greatest works of thought and art have been born in silence and solitude, the necessary accompaniments of imagination and vision. However gregarious we may be, we cannot know ourselves without the solitude and silence demanded by the soul. There is no need to escape from the world, but to enjoy it better we should leave some space for periods of reflective peace.

CHAPTER FIVE

Just Live Right

Walt Whitman tending the injured during the American Civil War

*There is a small piece of cinematic footage of Tolstoy
taken near the end of his life by an intrepid film-maker.
Tolstoy wouldn't let him in the house, but bounced up and down
on his doorstep crying: "Just live right!"*

HENRY SHUKMAN

How should we behave in response to the present time? Of course, the question is hardly a new one; generation after generation has faced decadence and tumult, and found its answers—answers invariably guided by a strong religious belief.

Is it any different today? I think so. In most European countries there has been a massive decline of faith. A commensurate growth of anxiety about the future of the environment has also led to widespread worries about climate change, environmental degradation and growth of population. So the question with which I began this chapter, the behaviour appropriate for a society which is losing its traditional moral guidelines, is destroying its environment and squandering its future resources, is not an academic one. It calls for an answer.

For potential clues I have chosen to look at the lives and work of a small number of exceptional people, whose deepest instinct in the face of the violence and destruction of their time is instructive: it was to respond with an affirmation of everything that for them made life worth living. All of them lived creatively and without resource to distraction; their work was focused, peaceful and humane. None was fanatical, none greedy, none overtly selfish; all saw it as their business to act with compassion towards nature and fulfil their natural talent.

VIRGIL AND A CIVIL WAR

Spiritus intus alit. (The spirit nourishes within.)
Virgil

My first choice is Virgil, most famous of Roman poets. He lived at a time of great disturbance, possibly even greater than our own. Yet what I admire apart from his verse is his dedication to study and to work when his world was falling apart.

He was born in 70 BC near Mantua in northern Italy, where his parents owned a farm. He was a middle-class child and a Roman citizen by birth. When he was about seventeen, he headed for Rome. Though he early made friends with many important Romans, among them the young Octavius who was afterwards to become the Emperor Augustus, Virgil was not drawn to the glamour of the capital; he preferred a quiet life in the countryside. It is known that he was very shy, often in poor health, and preferred a life of study and meditation. He was an intense student of poetry and of history, a bookish man whose ideal was to love the rivers and the woods, unhonoured in his way of life.

Having returned to the Mantuan farm, he began writing the first of his three celebrated literary works, all in verse. This was a collection of pastoral poems, known as the *Bucolics* or the *Eclogues*, a great book of poetry that two thousand years have not in any way diminished. Virgil's *Eclogues* were Spencer's and Milton's starting point in poetry, and Shakespeare in his comedies constantly returned to them. They were presented to the world in 37 or 36 BC, and swiftly became an enormous popular success.

The next publication was the *Georgics* in four books. It is about 2,186 lines long, and seems to have been written during the great climactic civil war which ended the disturbed period following the murder of Caesar in March 44 BC and the battle of Philippi in 42 BC. It contains practical advice to farmers about crops, trees, and animals, especially bees. There is a whole book on bee-keeping, an image of human life, orderly and public-spirited. In the *Georgics* Virgil also instructs on trees, with emphasis on the fruitfulness and responsiveness of nature. Thus sowing and reaping, with hard work, were for him part of a moral picture of the good life lived in harmony with nature.

The *Georgics* were finished in 29 BC and Virgil devoted the rest of his life to the composition of the *Aeneid*, a legendary narrative about the imagined origin of the Roman nation in times long before the foundation of Rome itself. It is probably the most widely known of all secular books in Europe from Roman days to our own. The poet died in 19 BC—the year in which the Pont du Gard near Nîmes was finished.

Virgil lived through an exceptional period of tumult and civil war. He was born in the year in which Pompey and Crassus forced their way into the consulship, was seven when Cataline fell fighting at the head of a revolutionary army opposing the Roman legions, was twenty six when Caesar was assassinated, and lived through the ensuing civil war. In the two years 42–41 BC, a hundred-and-fifty senators and two thousand equites (Roman soldiers who could afford to keep a horse) died in the wars and purges.

It is also a fact that of the fifty-one years of Virgil's life, sixteen were years of unprecedented civil disorder, during which considerable areas of Italy were devastated by fighting, famine and the forcible expropriation of land. A recent calculation has estimated that at that time a quarter of the land of Italy changed hands in the proscriptions and evictions. As late as 19 BC, the year of his death, there were serious riots in Rome.

Virgil's own farm was one of the many confiscated by discharged soldiers of the enormous armies then looking for their reward. Thereafter he went to live on a property near Naples where the emperor Augustus had granted him a residence.

I like to think of this scholarly man, surrounded by disorder, violence and lawlessness, writing about farming, about peaceful goodness, humanity and reconciliation. For him, like Archbishop Desmond Tutu, the ideas of reconciliation and harmony amounted to an obsession.

Virgil was also sensitive and sympathetic to all points of view and all kinds of people, even wicked ones. "He was not content to give only one side of a question," writes W. F. Jackson Knight in the introduction to his translation of the *Aeneid*. "Indeed, he often needed to express the truth about people or things when the truth itself looked paradoxical or even illogical, and probably no one but he could have shown the underlying sense." Virgil writes that it is not only by heroic champions in battle that valour is shown, but through courageous fidelity and resolute will in respect of more peaceful affairs.

Retreat from the battlefield of life, working in solitude, in pursuit of a creative end, is one answer to the problem of living when things fall apart.

MONTAIGNE DURING THE FRENCH WARS OF RELIGION

The man who knows how to enjoy his existence as he ought has attained to an absolute perfection, like that of the gods. We seek other conditions because we do not understand the proper use of our own, and go out of ourselves because we do not know what is within us. So it is no good our mounting on stilts, for even on stilts we have to walk with our own legs; and upon the most exalted throne in the world it is still our own bottom that we sit upon.

The finest lives are, in my opinion, those which conform to the common and human model in an orderly way, with no marvels and no extravagances.
Michel de Montaigne

Retreat was also a choice which the essayist Michel de Montaigne (1533–1592) practised for the last years of his life. As a young man he played an active role in the public world of his time: he was a counsellor to the Parlement of Bordeaux and twice elected that city's Mayor (in 1581 and 1583). Yet as a local politician (mostly despite his own desire), Montaigne refused to take sides in the bitter upheaval of those deeply divided years, the civil wars between the Huguenots and the Catholics that raged in France during the 16th and 17th centuries. In the terrible massacre that took place in Paris on the eve of St Bartholomew in 1572 (the year in which Montaigne retired) it is reported that between 3,000 and 4,000 fell; elsewhere the savagery was no less bloody. Montaigne had no illusions about the brutalities released by the Reformation.

How do we live in the midst of such turmoil?, he must have asked himself. Well, if we cannot accept inherited beliefs we can accept things as they come to us and simply enjoy them for what they are. For this, he paraphrases the scepticism of Ecclesiastes: "Receive things thankfully," says the Preacher, "in the aspect and taste that they are offered to thee, from day to day; the rest is beyond thy knowledge." Montaigne valued these truly sensible words so much that he had them inscribed on the ceiling of his library.

In 1571, when he was 38, he retired to his handsome castle at Montaigne, some 30 miles east of Bordeaux. Here he settled with his wife, his daughter, his staff and their animals. He built himself a circular library on the third floor of a tower at one corner of the castle. The library had three windows, a desk, a chair, and about a thousand books on philosophy, poetry, religion and history. As he read his favourite authors, he jotted down ideas which were later developed in his essays, the first two volumes of which were published in 1580, the third in 1588.

In these essays, characterised by tolerance and a lack of dogmatism ("I would willingly carry a candle in one hand for St Michael and a candle for his Dragon in the other"), the greatest humanist of the mid-sixteenth century sets out in language at once unsensational and intimate to discover the greatest of all prizes—self-knowledge—and through this, knowledge of all other men and women. "Every man bears the whole Form of the human condition," he wrote.

The essays reveal their author as a man of insatiable intellectual curiosity, kindly and wise, condemning bigotry, and sceptical in the sense that he denied that anything was either certain or even probable. For him no 'truth' was ever final, which was all the more exceptional in an age filled with those who knew that they, and they alone, had the truth, direct from God. We have a religion, he wrote, because "We happen to have been born in a country where it was in practice. . . . We regard its antiquity or the authority of the men who have maintained it (and) we fear the threats it fastens on unbelievers."

Montaigne was enlightened in other ways. He argued that humans are not in any way superior to animals; in fact quite the contrary. On one occasion when he was playing with his cat, he wondered whether the cat was not perhaps playing with him.

Montaigne is one of my (rather few) heroes. I think of him in that turbulent century, a contemplative working in solitude, outwardly conforming, inwardly free, a tolerant sceptic in an age of hatred and fundamentalist intolerance. There he is writing about every subject under the sun—his meals, his stools, his farts, cannibals, friendship, smells—when in other places men were consumed by the confident madness of their particular faith. In his quiet library Michel de Montaigne came to see that to philosophise is to learn how to live.

WALT WHITMAN NURSES THE WOUNDED OF THE AMERICAN CIVIL WAR

> I believe a leaf of grass is no less than the journey-work of the stars,
> And the pismire is equally perfect, and a grain of sand, and the egg
>   of the wren,
> And the tree-toad is a chef-d'oeuvre for the highest,
> And the running blackberry would adorn the parlours of heaven.
> And the narrowest hinge in my hand puts to scorn all machinery,
> And the cow crunching with depress'd head surpasses any statue,
> And a mouse is miracle enough to stagger sextillions of infidels.
> *Walt Whitman, from 'Song of Myself'*

The American poet Walt Whitman (1819–92), a contemporary of Tennyson, offers another contribution to my question: how to live with integrity when one's world has gone insane, how to remain true to oneself when the majority behave with the kind of blind amorality which, for example, infected the German and Japanese nations in the thirties and forties of the last century. Whitman was born on Long Island, New York, the son of a radical, free-thinking farmer. He had various jobs: beginning as a lawyer's errand boy, he worked in a printing office, then as a schoolteacher. Later, he edited two newspapers, and built and sold wooden houses. He never left America.

As he worked, he made notes for a series of poems which he had been long pondering. They were to be new, under no influence from the past. "Poet," he once wrote, "beware lest your poems are made in the Spirit, that comes from the study of pictures of things—and not from the Spirit that comes from the contact of real things themselves."

Whitman himself never lost contact with real things. His poems, written in free unrhyming lines, express the whole spirit of 19th-century America, its optimism, its energy and self-confidence. His subjects—the comradeship of men, the pride of craftsmanship, democracy, sex—portray the whole fabric of poor working men's lives. Yet the impression his poetry leaves is one of insolent bravado, abounding vitality and compassion for humanity.

At the outbreak of the Civil War, Whitman was 42 years old. He vowed to live a "purged" and "cleansed" life, wrote freelance journalism and visited the wounded in the hospitals in and around New York. A year later he travelled to Washington DC to care for his brother who had been wounded in the battle of Fredericksburg, in which some 18,000 soldiers had been killed. (In all, more than 10,000 military actions of one kind or another took place during the Civil war, but only a few like Vicksburg and Gettysburg, with its 51,000 casualties, were big battles.)

In Washington he continued to spend his spare time as a volunteer nurse, visiting both wounded Confederate and Union soldiers and offering his usual "cheer and magnetism" to alleviate some of the mental depression and bodily suffering he saw in the wards. During this period Whitman carried a tiny notebook in which he would note the needs and wants of the wounded—for example raspberry syrup, rice pudding, a note paper and pencil—or the addresses of the soldiers' families to whom he would write on behalf of the wounded or, in some cases, the deceased. The exertion, exposure and strain of these years left him a shattered and prematurely aged man.

Nonetheless, Whitman continued to write poetry with unceasing vigour. In 1855 he self-published the first edition of his great collection, *Leaves of Grass*, subsequently adding to it the poems written at a later date. Once praised by Emerson, it made him famous. Whitman's poetry, like his character, was imbued with his gigantic egotism and refusal to be yoked by cultural sophistications. He was, like Montaigne, Cézanne, Hildegard de Bingen, Henry David Thoreau and Harlan Hubbard, entirely his own man.

MIRACLES

Why, who makes much of a miracle?
As for me I know of nothing else but miracles,
Whether I walk the streets of Manhattan,
Or dart my sight over the roofs of houses toward the sky,
Or wade with naked feet along the beach just in the edge of the water,
Or stand under trees in the woods,
Or talk by day with anyone I love, or sleep in the bed at night with any
    one I love,
Or sit at table at dinner with the rest,
Or look at strangers opposite me riding in the car,
Or watch honey-bees busy around the hide of a summer fore-noon,
Or animals feeding in the fields,
Or birds, or the wonderfulness of insects in the air,
Or the wonderfulness of the sundown, or of stars shining so quiet and bright,
Or the exquisite delicate thin curve of the new moon in spring.
These with the rest, one and all, are to me miracles,
The whole referring, yet each distinct and in its place.

To me every hour of the light and dark is a miracle,
Every cubic inch of space is a miracle,
Every square yard of the surface of the earth is spread the same.
Every foot of the interior swarms with the same.
To me the sea is a continual miracle,
The fishes that swim—the rocks—the motion of the waves—the ships with
    men in them,
What stranger miracles are there?

YUSUF ISLAM AND THE ORPHANS OF WAR

I'd just like to live in a tree hut,
Yes I'd just like to live in a tree hut,
Yes I'd just like to live in a tree hut and
Listen to the sounds of the birds.
Cat Stevens

Another tireless worker for sanity is Steven Demetre Georgiou (born 1948), better known as Cat Stevens and now as Yusuf Islam. Georgiou was the son of a Swedish mother and a Greek Cypriot father who ran a busy restaurant in the theatre land district of London. By the age of 19, as a popular song writer and singer of Top Ten hits, he had reinvented himself as Cat Stevens. In this capacity he went on to become one of the biggest solo artist of the 1960s and 70s, composing such classics as 'Matthew and Son', 'I Love My Dog' and 'Teaser and the Firecat', winning 8 Gold Discs and selling over 50 million LPs.

As a celebrity the singer enjoyed fame and wealth, but also suffered from something more demanding—long schedules and constant contractual pressures for new songs and albums. "Although I lived the fast life," he says, "I was always searching for answers. I was aware that there was something I had to achieve in life. At first I thought that if I had luxuries that would answer all my problems, but it didn't."

In 1969, following a bout of tuberculosis which hospitalised him for a year—"I felt I was on the brink of death. . . . I needed a break so that I could review my life and decide where I wanted to go and not necessarily where my agent felt I should go"—he undertook an ongoing search for peace, an endeavour exacerbated by a near-death experience when a freak wave off the coast of Manila sucked him under and far out to sea. At that moment, believing he was destined to drown, he asked God to help him and, in return, promised to dedicate his life to His work.

Cat Stevens survived, and in December 1977, after reading the Koran, he walked away from the frenetic world of rock to start a life based on his new faith as a Muslim. "The moment I became a Muslim, I found peace," he says, "I never wanted to be a star." Six months later he changed his name to Yusuf Islam.

Then, much to the dismay of his many fans, he abandoned performance. For nearly twenty years he simply disappeared. He married, had five children, and immersed himself in the devout procedures of his religion. As a multi-millionaire, Yusuf Islam could have lived the luxurious and indulgent life of a former celebrity, but instead he chose to devote himself to the relief of suffering. He set up an international relief organisation, Muslim Aid, to assist the famine in Africa. In 1990 he joined a delegation of British Muslims and went to Iraq on a peace mission, negotiating successfully for the release of four hostages. Meanwhile the charity constructed emergency shelters and sent aid to thousands of refugees displaced through the Bosnian homicide and 'ethnic cleansing'.

Later, Yusuf Islam set up another charity, Small Kindness, to alleviate the suffering of families, and especially orphans made homeless by conflict. In Iraq, this charity has been one of the few organisations to remain active, with the rising number of children orphaned by the war. In addition, he has donated large sums of his own money to fund victims of the September 11th attacks in New York, and has been actively involved in the negotiations to free British hostages.

Since 1994, Yusuf Islam has returned to the creative side of his talent, releasing a further 10 albums. He has also returned to the stage to perform for the Mandela AIDS Benefit Concert in Cape Town. Since the beginning of 2005, Small Kindness has delivered £50,000 to help those whose lives were devastated by the tsunami disaster. "I think back to the time that I, myself, was helplessly sinking in the vast waves of the Pacific Ocean and that it was no one other than God who was able to save me." More recently he has expressed his horror at the "nightmarish acts of carnage" inflicted on Londoners on 7th July 2005.

WANGARI MAATHAI PLANTS 20 MILLION TREES

Too often when we talk about conservation, we don't think about culture. But during our work with the Green Belt Movement, we realised that some of the communities had lost aspects of their culture that facilitated conservation of the environment. Culture defines who we are and how we see ourselves. A new attitude toward nature provides space for a new attitude toward culture and the role it plays in sustainable development.

Mount Kenya, Africa's second highest peak, is a World Heritage Site. It is topped by glaciers and is the source of many of Kenya's rivers. Now, partly because of climate change and partly because of logging and encroachment due to crop cultivation, the glaciers are melting. Many of the rivers flowing from the mountain have dried up or their levels have declined. Biological diversity is threatened as the forests fall. Mount Kenya used to be sacred to the Kikuyu people. If the mountain was still given the reverence the culture accorded it, people would not have allowed illegal logging and clear-cutting in the forests. Cultural revival might be the only thing that stands between conservation or destruction of the environment.

Wangari Maathai

The leading Kenyan environmentalist, civil rights activist and deputy environment minister in the Kenyan government, Wangari Maathai, was born in Nyeri, Kenya, in 1940. In 1960 she won a Kennedy scholarship to study in America, earned a master's degree in biology from the University of Pittsburgh, and became the first woman in East Africa to acquire a Ph.D.

Returning to her homeland six years later, Wangari Maathai was dismayed to discover the degradation of the forests and the farmland caused by deforestation, corruption and poor land management. Heavy rains had washed away much of the topsoil, silt had clogged the rivers, and fertilisers were depriving the soil of its natural organic nutrients. With her doctorate in biological science, Maathai knew that the planting of trees could radically improve the soil quality and change women's lives for the better. It was, she saw, a women's issue. She therefore decided to help solve the problem by planting trees.

Under the auspices of the National Council of Women of Kenya, of which she was the chair from 1981 to 1987, Wangari Maathai introduced the idea of planting trees through citizen foresters, and called the method the Green Belt Movement. It was founded on Earth Day, 1977.

Through the Green Belt Movement, Wangari Maathai has assisted women in planting more than 20 million trees (with an estimated 70 percent survival rate) on their farms and on schools and church compounds in Kenya and all over East Africa.

Yet her path to success was by no means an easy one. During the

1970s and 1980s she came under scrutiny and vilification from the government of Daniel arap Moi, and suffered physical attacks and imprisonment. Nonetheless Wangari refused to compromise her belief that local people rather than corrupt officials were best trusted to look after their own resources.

Today, her situation has radically changed. She is the recipient of numerous awards including the 2004 Nobel Peace Prize for her "stand at the front of the fight to promote ecologically viable social, economic and cultural developments in Kenya and Africa". In 2003 Maathai was also elected to Parliament by an overwhelming 98 percent of the vote, where she is currently the Assistant Secretary for Environment, Wildlife and Natural Resources in the democratically elected government of President Mwai Kibaki.

Her life is an example of how one person can turn around the lives of thousands, if not millions, of others, by empowering them to help themselves.

TOUCHING PEACE AND STILLNESS:
SERVICE, EXPRESSION, SILENCE

The individuals I have selected to describe may be few—too few, perhaps—but they are representative of all those who have turned adversity to advantage, hate to love, the negative to its opposite. The pattern of their lives is important because it can provide an inspiration for others also seeking to achieve some kind of sanity in a world that at certain times and places can give the appearance of having gone mad.

To achieve this end, none of them massed together, followed the crowd, worked to the point of insensibility, were drugged by consumerism or, like millions of others, raised their arms in salute to a Führer; they remained single-minded, free and dignified. They lived true to themselves. Furthermore, all of them knew that silence was the best preparation for the reception of inspirations and a life of action.

They lived at different times, had differing backgrounds, natures and aims; yet, I suspect, they had in common a number of distinguishing values and patterns of behaviour. These, for the sake of clarity, I have linked under three major headings: service, expression, and silence.

Service

Currently, our society is dragging us along on a producing and consuming treadmill to the point where we are ceasing to remember our true needs. Our energies are dispersed, our witness diluted, our originality ignored, by the stresses of the commercial world; our culture leaves us with few opportunities to become either aware of our deeper nature or the dangers that lie ahead. It also prevents us from being present where we are: we neither see, nor hear, nor smell. At times such as this, an act of service to another being is of value—not only to the latter, but also to ourselves.

Yet the time and energy devoted to serving other people is, if deeply important, only one element of a life of service. There are other kinds: for example service to animals, trees, the Earth.

Service to the Earth may be as insignificant as feeding birds with nuts each morning, limiting the use of the car, growing our own food, reducing our carbon output, recycling our domestic refuse and planting a tree. Or it might be more strenuous, such as a public resistance to all that seeks to damage, violate and plunder the natural order.

Expression

It has been observed that some of those I singled out for admiration, Virgil for example, may have turned their backs on the life of their time, and to a lesser extent their families and friends, to give undivided attention to their own creative work. Richard Wagner, Marcel Proust, Henri Matisse, amongst countless others, were also single-minded in their commitment to the expression and development of a personal vision. It is a charge of selfishness that can be laid at the door of countless creative artists, and those bent on a religious vocation, too.

Personally, I don't see it that way. We are all born with a creative (and religious) nature, and its expression—more insistent in some than in others—is one of the more important obligations of our lives. Often painful, nearly always strenuous, demanding of time and effort, frequently challenged by others, sometimes producing no apparent rewards, the practice of creativity is to be welcomed, never denied. For the person who seeks to discover and give expression to himself or herself may be the very one to discover some new insight, some fresh vision of ultimate benefit to other people. It can also be an expression of praise.

Silence

By silence, solitude and slowness, I mean more than the mere absence of sound, other people and speed, important as these can also be; I mean what arises from the generative root of all three: prayer and inspiration, stillness and joy, emptiness, creativity, solace, praise. It seems to me that each of these may possess the power to contribute an effective antidote to the distraction, the restlessness and triviality of the present time.

"The destruction of the human race can only be avoided," says Thich Nhat Hanh, "by finding a new cultural direction in which the spiritual dimension plays the role of guide." That direction, whatever form it takes, must surely arise from the ground of silence, solitude and slowness.

Silence, solitude and slowness are indispensable to those who seek to become more alive to the existence of the present moment, the only reality we are privileged to know. They are needed because they give order and harmony to the apparent confusion of the contingent world, they provide us with a solid centre in what might otherwise appear as almost chaos. Through silence, solitude and slowness we can rise to face the struggle for life and keep our confidence in the future, whatever pains it holds, intact.

NOTES

CHAPTER ONE

1. George Orwell originally wrote: "(Theirs) is a rather restless, culture-less life centring around tinned food, *Picture Post*, the radio and the combustion engine. It is a civilisation in which children grow up with an intimate knowledge of magnetos and in complete ignorance of the Bible. To that civilisation belong the people who are most at home in, and most definitely of, the modern world, the technicians and the higher-paid skilled workers, the airmen and their mechanics, the radio experts, film producers, popular journalists and industrial chemists."

CHAPTER TWO

2. Antoni Gaudí (1852–1926), architect of many buildings in Barcelona including the unfinished Sagrada Familia; the Romanian sculptor, Constantin Brancusi (1876–1957); the French painter Georges Braque (1882–1963) and the Italian avant-garde composer, Luigi Nono (1924–1990). There are also the English painters Gwen John and Cecil Collins.

CHAPTER THREE

3. "These findings are confirmed by Francis Green, professor of economics at the University of Kent, who writes that there has been a significant downturn in job satisfaction since the early 1990s. The number of people who rated their job 'very' or 'completely' satisfying has fallen by 10 percentage points across the decade. "People are dissatisfied with the work itself. It's not about the financial rewards, but the day to day experience of how we carry out work tasks. People feel that they have to work harder . . . They feel that they are on the go all day and that contributes to more stress. And they are recording that they have less control and autonomy over their daily tasks. There are more targets, more rules, less trust."

From 'It's definitely not the job for lots of people', a report by Sean Coughlan in *The Guardian*, 30th October 2004.

BIBLIOGRAPHY

Ryuichi Abe and Peter Asked, *Great Fool: Zen Master Ryokan: Poems, Letters, and other Writing,* University of Hawai Press, Honolulo, 1996.

Robert Aitken, *Taking the Path of Zen,* North Point Press, 1982.

Christopher Bamford, *Negative Capability,* Parabola, Volume 30, No.2.

Stephen Batchelor, *Buddhism without Beliefs: A Contemporary Guide to Awakening,* Bloomsbury, 1997.

Wendell Berry, *Harlan Hubbard: Life and Work,* The University Press of Kentucky, 1990.

Vinoba Bhave, *Talks on the Gita,* Sarva-Seva-Sangh-Prakashan, 1981.

Ronald Blythe, *The Circling Year,* The Canterbury Press, 2001.

Fiona Bowie & Oliver Davies, *Hildegard de Bingen: An Anthology,* SPCK, 1990.

David Cadman, *Eternal Wisdom in an Age of Illusion: Reflections Upon a Pathway,* a paper prepared for the Annual Baháí'i Lecture Maryland, USA, 2003.

Isabel Colgate, *A Pelican in the Wilderness: Hermits, Solitaries and Recluses,* Harper Collins, 2002.

John Daniel, *Rogue River Journal: a winter alone,* Shoemaker & Hoard 2005.

Esther de Waal, *The Celtic Vision; Selections from the Carmina Gadelica,* Darton, Longman and Todd, 1990.

Jared Diamond, *Collapse: How Societies Choose to Fail or Survive,* Allen Lane, 2005.

Annie Dillard, *Pilgrim at Tinker Creek,* various editions.

Diana L. Eck, *Darsan: Seeing the Divine in India,* Anima Books, 1985.

Patrick Leigh Fermor, *Time to Keep Silence,* Penguin Books, 1988.

Matthew Fox, *Illuminations of Hildegard de Bingen,* Bear and Company, 1985.

Matthew Fox, ed, *Hildegard de Bingen's Book of Divine Works,* Bear and Company, 1987.

Erich Fromm, *The Sane Society,* Routledge and Kegan Paul, 1963.

Erich Fromm, *To Have and to Be,* Jonathan Cape, 1976.

Monica Furlong, *Merton: A Biography,* Harper and Row, 1980.

Edward Goldsmith, *The Way: An Ecological World View,* Themis Books, 1996.

John Gray, *Straw Dogs: Thoughts on Humans and Other Animals,* Granta Books, 2002.

Ernst-Gerhard Guse and Franz Armin Morat, *Giorgio Morandi,* Prestel, 1999.

Rene Guénon, *The Reign of Quantity & The Signs of the Times,* Penguin Books, 1972.

Dolf Hartsuiker, *Sadhus: Holy Men of India,* Thames and Hudson, 1993.

Carl Honoré, *In Praise of Slow: How a Worldwide Movement is Challenging the Cult of Speed,* Orion, 2004.

Adrian House, *Francis of Assisi,* Pimlico, 2001.

Harlan Hubbard, *Shantyboat: A River way of Life,* The University Press of Kentucky, 1977.

Harlan Hubbard, *Life on the fringe of society: Payne Hollow,* Thomas Y. Crowell Company, 1974.

Harlan Hubbard, *Payne Hollow Journal,* The University Press of Kentucky, 1996.

Robert Hughes, *Nothing If Not Critical,* The Harvill Press, 1990.

Aldous Huxley, *The Perennial Philosophy,* Chatto and Windus, 1946.

Steven Johnson, *Everything Bad is Good for You: How Popular Culture is Making us Smarter,* Allen Lane, 2005.

Thomas H. Johnson, ed., *The Complete Poems of Emily Dickinson,* Faber and Faber, 1970.

John Keats, *Selected Letters,* ed. Robert Gittings, Oxford University Press, 2002.

Connie Ann Kirk, *Emily Dickinson: A Biography*, Greenwood Press, 2004.

James Howard Kunstler, *The Long Emergency: Surviving the Converging Catastrophes of the Twenty-First Century*, Atlantic Monthly Press, 2005.

John Lane, *Timeless Simplicity,* Green Books, 2001.

John Lane, *Timeless Beauty,* Green Books, 2003.

Lawrence LeShan, *How to Meditate,* Wildwood House, 1976.

James Lovelock, *The Revenge of Gaia*, Allen Lane, 2006.

Peter Levi, *the Frontiers of Paradise: A study of Monks & Monastries,* Collins Harvill, 1988.

Peter Levi, *Virgil: His Life and Times,* Duckworth, 1998.

Charles Mackay, *Extraordinary Popular Delusions and the Madness of Crowds,* Wordsworth Reference, 1995.

Juan Mascara, trans., *The Dhammapada,* Penguin Books, 1973.

Jeffrey Masson, *The Nine Emotional Lives of Cats,* Vintage, 2003.

Peter Matthiessen, *The Snow Leopard,* Chatto and Windus, 1979.

Rollo May, *The Courage to Create,* Collins, 1976.

Thomas Merton, *The Silent Life,* Sheldon Press, 1957.

Thomas Merton, *Thoughts in Solitude,* Burns and Oates, 1958.

Thomas Merton, *Zen and the Birds of Appetite,* New Directions, 1968.

Michel de Montaigne, *Essays,* various editions.

Thomas Moore, *Care of the Soul,* Harper Collins, 1992.

Toshiharu Oseko, *Basho's Haiku,* Toshiharu Oseko, 1990.

Max Picard, *The World of Silence,* The Harvard Press, 1950.

Bill Porter, *Road to Heaven: Encounters with Chinese Hermits,* Mercury House, San Francisco, 1993.

John Cowper Powys, *The Art of Happiness,* The Bodley Head, 1935.

Llewelyn Powys, *Love and Death,* The Bodley Head, 1939.

Marcel Proust, *Remembrance of Things Past,* Penguin Books, 1983.

Knud Rasmussen, *Songs and Stories of the Netsilik Eskimos,* Glydendahl (Copenhagen), 1931.

Martin Rees, *Our Final Century,* William Heinmann, 2003.

John Rewald, *Paul Cézanne: A Biography,* Thames and Hudson, 1986.

Robert D. Richardson, *Henry Thoreau: A Life of the Mind,* University of California Press, 1995.

Jean-François Rischard, *High Noon: 20 Global Issues, 20 years to Solve Them,* The Perseus Press, 2002.

Nancy Wilson Ross, *Hinduism, Buddhism, Zen,* Faber and Faber, 1968.

George B. Sansom, *Japan: A Short Cultural History,* Charles E. Tuttle, 1931.

Heinrich Schipperges, *The World of Hildegard de Bingen: Her Life, Times and Visions,* Burns and Oates, 1998.

Richard B. Sewell, *The Life of Emily Dickinson,* Farrar, Straus and Giroux, 1974.

Henryk Skolimowski, *Eco Yoga,* Gaia Books, 2004.

Pitirim A. Sorokin, *The Crisis of Our Age,* World Publications, 1992.

John Stevens, *One Robe, One Bowl: The Zen Poetry of Ryokan,* Weatherall, 1977.

Anthony Storr, *Solitude: A Return to the Self*, Harper Collins, 1997.

Shunryu Suzuki, *Zen Mind, Beginner's Mind*, John Wetherall, 1970.

Daisetz T. Suzuki, *Zen and Japanese Culture*, Princeton University Press, 1959.

Brian Swimme, *The Hidden Heart of the Cosmos*, Orbis Books, 1996.

Michel Terrace, *Bonnard at Le Cannet*, Thames and Hudson, 1988.

Wilfred Thesiger, *Arabian Sands*, Penguin Books, 1980.

Thich Nhat Hanh, *Our Appointment With Life*, Parallax Press, 1990.

Thich Nhat Hanh, *The Miracle of Mindfulness: A Manual on Meditation*, Beacon Press, 1987.

Thich Nhat Hanh, *Zen Keys*, Doubleday, 1974.

Henry David Thoreau, *Journal*, Dover Publications, 1962.

Henry David Thoreau, *Walden and Civil Disobedience*, various editions.

John E. Thornes, *John Constable's Skies*, The University of Birmingham Press, 1999.

Thorstein Veblen, *Conspicious Consumption*, Penguin Books, 2005.

Virgil, *The Eclogues, The Georgics*, trans by C. Day Lewis, Oxford University Press, 1983.

Virgil, *The Aeneid*, trans W. F. Jackson Knight, Penguin Books, 1988.

Jasper Walljasper, *A Hurried History of Time*, Resurgence, no 201.

Max Weber, *The Protestant Ethic and the Spirit of Capitalsism*, Unwin University Books, 1971.

Ludwig Wittgenstein, *Tractatus Logico-Philosophicus*, Routledge and Kegan Paul, 1949.

George Woodcock, *Thomas Merton, Monk and Poet*, Farrar, Straus & Giroux, 1978.

Compact Discs

Hildegard of Bingen:
A Feather on the Breath of God, Gothic Voices, Hyperion.
Symphoniae. Sequentia, Deutsche Harmonia Mundi.
Ordo virtutum. Sequentia, Deutsche Harmonia Mundi.
Canticles of Esctasy, Sequentia, Harmonia Mundi.